I0223325

THE WAY

MORE SPIRIT FROM THE WELL

THE WAY

MORE SPIRIT FROM THE WELL

A way of life for the modern world
based on the teachings of the ancient wisdom
&
my mentor Eugene Halliday

by
Philip Rose

Melchisedec Press

Melchisedec Press

5 Taylor Road, Altrincham, Cheshire WA14 4LR
melchisedecpress.net
info@melchisedecpress.net
philoldford5@gmail.com

Published in the UK in 2021 by Melchisedec Press

All text and illustrations by Philip Rose
Edited by Hephzibah Yohannan

The rights of Philip Rose have been asserted by him in accordance with
Copyright Designs and Patents Act.

© Philip Rose & Hephzibah Yohannan

The moral right of the author is asserted.

Cover design
© Philip Rose & Hephzibah Yohannan

The book titles were previously published individually by The Rose Studio

All rights reserved. No part of this publication may be reproduced, stored in
a retrieval system or transmitted in any form or by any means without the prior
permission in writing of the publisher, nor be otherwise circulated in any form of
binding or cover other than that in which it is published without a similar
condition, including this condition, being imposed on the subsequent purchaser.

ISBN 978-1-872240-48-0 (hardback)
ISBN 978-1-872240-49-7 (paperback)
ISBN 978-1-872240-50-3 (ebook)

A CIP catalogue record for this book is available from the British Library

Printed and bound by Ingram Spark
Set in Baskerville

Sail forth, pilgrim, sail forth
From out your inner sea
Into the wildest deepest ocean.

Seek the still centre: once found, stay there.

Dedication

For my dear departed wife Elizabeth with whom I shared sixty-seven years of loving companionship. As Thea Rose she is the author of *Mindshift: With Eyes Half Closed*

CONTENTS

Foreword

This book brings together a further collection of short books published over a number of years by Philip Rose. They detail his lifelong search for the meaning of life, his meeting with his friend and mentor Eugene Halliday, and his deep spiritual experiences when alone at sea. An actor, artist, writer, and family man, Philip is also a solo trans-Atlantic yachtsman.

Now aged 96, Philip is still writing to express and share his spiritual philosophy drawn from many years of study and meditation. His expression, in simple language, of his experiences, at the same time both human and transcendent, conveys the heart of that state of being, described and taught in the most precise language by Eugene Halliday, in his book Reflexive Self-Consciousness.

This book ends with a series of Sonnets which are a distillation of Philip's life experience and his many years of internal work.

Hephzibah Yohannan 2021

Acknowledgements

For this second volume of my collected works, *The Way: More Spirit from the Well*, I extend my grateful thanks to my three faithful friends Hephzibah, Cheree in Canada, and Ruth; and to my dear brother Douglas and his wife Dorothy in Australia who have always encouraged and given me strength to keep writing. Also to Margaret Littler and Sheila Taylor who have typed sections of the book; to Sheila and Robert Taylor who have proofread the whole; and to John Zaradin who has painstakingly prepared the book for printing.

This collection of my books has been brought together and published here by the Melchisedec Press, which was founded by David Mahlowe to publish the work of Eugene Halliday. The Melchisedec Press is now edited by Hephzibah Yohannan, Eugene Halliday's literary and artistic executor, with whom I hereby share the copyright of my work.

Philip Rose 2021

Introduction: The Purpose of Life

The Purpose of Life. This is simple. The purpose of Life is the return to the cause of Life. What Life is, is in its Essence unknowable. To our limited perceptions it seems to be an awareness of itself. Simply awareness aware of itself. As such, it seems to, so to speak, project out from itself, to bud out as a seed, to bloom as a flower, discover what it is in itself, mature and develop itself to its optimum, then slowly fade and sleep — or, as we would say, die — and then after evaluating the results, wake and begin the whole process again. A new universe thus arises. This goes on infinitely without beginning or end. The movement is circular, ever spiralling upwards, or from the opposite viewpoint, downwards, an hourglass endlessly turning. Thus Life is, has always been, will always be.

The purpose of life for us humans is the return to the cause of life. This means, as the theologians would say, the return to God, or as the mystics would say, the return of the individual being to the universal cosmic being that is the origin of life and is, in fact, life itself. Plotinus calls it 'The flight of the Alone to the Alone', a beautiful poetic way of putting it.

The Gnostics say we are God acting in the place where we are, tiny sparks from his burning fire and so in principle identical in essence. The orthodox theologians say we are only of like nature but not identical.

If we are in essence God, why the need to return to Him? Because we are separated from Him. God, as such, is that formless, intelligent, awareness, that consciousness of himself that creates the universe, which is his projection of himself outwards into manifestation. He is his own body. That body he lives as an invisible presence, a spirit energising and giving it this mysterious power we call Life. He is that Life. He, as he is in himself, and He, as he is the Universe, are identical and yet not identical. He, as he is in himself, I call the Nothing, for He is not a thing: He, as he is the universe, I call the Something, for He is all things. This is a Paradox, and is a difficult concept to grasp. It is not One and yet not Two. The Sanscrit term is Advaita and is the basis behind the Hindu philosophy of the Vedanta. The Something and the Nothing, the same and yet not the same. In this paradox we exist. We are as cells, the somethings in that body which is ultimately noting. Each being is a sentient cell in the body of God, whether it be a mollusc, a tree, a flower, a stone, an animal or a human being. Everything is alive and aware and sentient of itself, from the greatest dimness to the greatest clarity. The highest

2

evolute on this planet is the human being, who is gifted not only with awareness, but also with self-awareness, the ability to reflect on his own origin.

So what is this Return? At a certain point the human being perceives itself as a separate being surrounded by other separate beings. As it grows and develops this sense of separateness increases. The process can be seen in the new born baby, growing into a child, then a youth or maid, the fully adult. The baby and child see the whole world as one, an indivisible wholeness with no separateness anywhere. As it grows this unity gradually fades until it becomes a multitude of separate things and beings, and the child has become an adult. Thus as the baby becomes an adult it loses its sense of unity and gains a sense of diversity. As a baby it is close to God: as an adult it is far from God.

So, the adult now fully considers itself a conscious being in its own right. It can experience all the delights and wonders of the external world. It now knows itself, as a separate being — a great gain — but it has lost its initial childish wonder. It has lost its wholeness. A drop of water feels itself as a drop of water, it may feel itself as that drop in the vastness of the ocean, but it does not reach its fullness of possibilities until it unifies itself with that ocean while still possessing its sense of identity. This is the purpose of life.

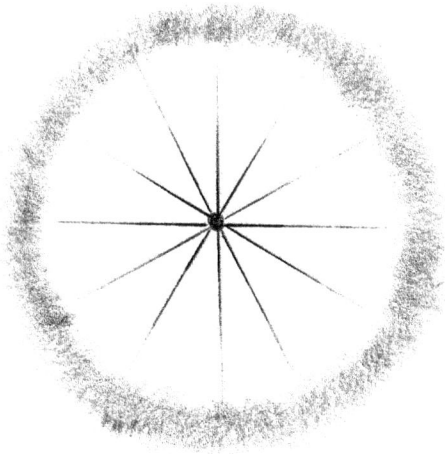

Book 1

SELF–REALISATION
(NOTHING SPECIAL)

Deny Love not — it may not come again

Philip Rose

1)   *Self–Realisation is the highest possible transcendental state of being possible to mankind at the present time.*

It is one with the Infinite Spirit which is the source of all things and which some call God. There is nothing other than this spirit. My mentor Eugene calls it Absolute Sentient Power (Asp).

2)   *Eugene calls this state Reflexive Self-Consciousnes (Resec)*

He says it is the only existing or possible instrument whereby the xelements of man's thought may be brought into correspondence with the elements of phenomenal and noumenal being. Without this correspondence, it is impossible for a man to understand the nature of his being and that of the universe at large. Without this correspondence man's mental processes must remain for ever out of phase with reality and in this out of phase state man must suffer physically, mentally and psychically ………. he is by that fact deprived of the wholeness essential to his perfect integration, without which integration permanent happiness and well-being are unattainable.

3) *Self–Realisation in its fullness can never be expressed in words*

It is utterly ineffable and must be experienced not intellectually understood. When this occurs the feeling and knowledge is one of absolute certainty. Peace and harmony sweep over one, both with oneself and with all creation. The overriding sensation is one of love, of absolute love, of love for oneself and for all of creation. There is no more fear, anxiety, worry and stress. One is in the `Peace that passes all understanding`. Surely this is `a consummation devoutly to be wished !`

4) *It occurs when the self identifies with the Self.*

The human being is usually regarded as a threefold one consisting of spirit, soul and body. It doesn`t have a soul it is a soul. It is a soul suspended between the spirit and the body These three are one, a single entity called the self. Considered separately the body, which includes the mind, or lower mind, is called the ego, The soul, which is the higher mind, is the true essence of the being. It can choose whether to identify with the spirit or the ego or both at once, in which case it has equilibrium, Normally it chooses to identify with the ego although it cannot ignore the spirit completely. If it chooses to identify with the spirit, which is the Supreme Identity (ASP) it can be said to be the self which is identified with the Self, When fully identified, when the self has fully surrendered to the Self, it is said to be Self-Realised. This state, which is unexplainable in words, sometimes reaches an intensity often called Ecstasy or Rapture.

5) *The enemy of Realisation is the ego.*

The ego is the enemy because it is subject externally to the temptations of the manifest world, internally to its own desires, which are normally of a love of and movement toward pleasure and a hatred of and a movement away from pain Both external and internal temptations are one for they are both in the mind. So the mind is the real enemy of realisation.

A problem now arises. The only way of overcoming the temptations is by use of the mind. But how can the mind overcome itself? It is a paradox. Here we meet the real problem of reaching Realisation. For it is all paradox. What can be done?

6) *Nothing needs to be done.*

One need do nothing for one is already there. One is already there for one has always been there. One is born perfect, all one has to do is realise it. One can realise it in an instant. Then why does no one do it. Because something stands in the way, a little thing called the Fall. This is the fall from original purity and innocence into materiality. The fall occurs when the being feels itself as a separate being from the world around it. A baby doesn`t feel this. For him everything is one and he is not separate from it. Thus he is perfect. As he grows he comes under the influence of his parents and teachers and gradually comes to sense, and realise, he is a separate being in his own right, and so begins the fall into temptations, both of the external world and the internal temptations of his newly arisen desires. He has forgotten his origin and so is no longer perfect. But deep inside is his true and real self which is still perfect and has always been and always will be perfect. As soon as he realises this he is a realised, an enlightened, being. But can he realise it ?

7) *What then must he do?*

Jesus said, "Of what use is it if a man gain the whole world and lose his own soul"? This means that for a man to gain his soul, i.e. his true essence at one with the Infinite Spirit, his higher mind. he must die to, or overcome or control, his lower mind, the mind subject to the temptations. This is the task, this is the difficult bit. But it is also the easy bit, at least in the early stages. There are two paths, the one is the normal path of the average man, the other is the path of the newly awakened man. All that is required is to prefer this second path. Just prefer to be realised. Don`t bother if it seems to be too difficult, just prefer that, rather than going on in the old way. Jesus called the first way the broad way that leads to damnation and the second way the narrow way that leads to life eternal. The simple preferring is all that`s required, for it releases forces that will eventually bring about the realisation. Strange things will begin to be perceived, a book will fall into your hands that is just what you need, you will meet a friend in the street you hadn't seen for ages who will suggest a meeting you should go to. Other odd things will happen that are of significance. Jung called them synchronicities. What is happening is that a power is now helping you. This power is the Infinite Spirit which is in and behind all phenomena, which is, so to speak, waiting for you to come along. For it wishes all the world to be realised, and helps all who are on the path. You will find things get harder as you proceed but conversely they get easier from the help as it increases flowing down from the spirit. Just be firm in your resolve and success is assured. (Actually of course it is your real self which has decided now is the time to cease its identification with the ego and reaffirm itself as its real self) Remember always to take it easy as you proceed. The next step will always occur spontaneously to you. (Believe all this as I speak from experience.)

8)   *The Non Dual.*

The principle of non-duality needs to be understood as it leads to an understanding of what realisation actually is. The manifest world is actually a dual world. Every phenomenon is seen in relation to its opposite. Good cannot exist without evil, up without down, right without left, etc. They are the two sides of the one coin. This coin is the Supreme Spirit, is Ultimate Reality. These two sides or opposites are known in the Chinese system of the Tao as the yin-yang, yin being the negative or female, yang the positive or male. They are not opposed to each other as is commonly supposed, on the contrary they are complementary to each other, for positive cannot exist without negative. Now here is the mystery. For when the positive and negative are brought together, as in electricity, the lamp lights up, lightning flashes, there is an explosion. Realisation occurs. The coin is realised in its entirety. Before, only one side or the other can be known, now it is the real thing. The Hindu philosophy of the Vedanta expresses this in the Sanscrit word of Advaita which means `not two, not one`. This apparently paradoxical statement expresses this difficult concept perfectly. For Reality is not the two sides of the coin, nor is it that which is in the middle, not two, not one. It is that which only occurs when the two and the one fuse and are seen as Reality while still remaining themselves. A certain leap of imagination is required to `get this`, but once you `get it` you are realised. No one can teach you this wisdom, you must find it in yourselves. Put as simply as I can, it means that on the one hand is the unknown `somewhat` that is the sentient origin of the world and usually known as God, and on the other is the visible manifested world which is expressed as a duality of complementary opposites. These are two expressions of the one reality which can only be understood as complementary to each other. The paradox is that the `somewhat`, God, remains always itself as the world always remains itself, while reality can only be understood when they are seen as one. Yet they are not one, for the `somewhat`, God, produces the world from itself as a means of, so to speak, seeing itself. The world is the reflection of God, as you can see yourself in the mirror. You in the mirror are you and yet it is only a reflection not the real you. In my previous booklets I call the unknown God the Nothing, while I call the manifested world the Something. The Nothing produces the Something out of itself, which is its reflection, its shadow. Your shadow is you and yet is not you and wherever you go your shadow goes with you. The two are one and yet not one. Baffling, yet that is the secret.

9)   Resec.

Eugene, in his short book of 50 pages Reflexive Self-Consciousness explains what the mind, consciousness, is. He says that everything is known by the mind and yet the mind itself is unknown. He says that to get Resec the key is his maxim that the Observer is not the Observed. When you observe something it is not you. You can observe everything but you can never observe yourself. The eye can never observe itself directly it can only observe its reflection. He then says that a good exercise is to say to yourself when you are observing something or considering an idea "It is the Self which is consciousness itself which is looking at this thing (or considering this idea). This Self I am. I return to the Self". This is a tremendously important statement. It involves the difference between reflect and reflex. Both words are derived from the Latin reflectare to bend or bend back. When observing or studying something, one must to a certain extent identify or sink into that something in order to understand it or, so to speak, come to terms with it. If one goes too far, or sinks too deep, then one goes under the laws governing that thing and so is one with that thing and so has lost one`s freedom to be oneself. One has become the reflection of that thing. In order to avoid this. Eugene says, before this can happen, "I am the Self, I return to the Self".

I reflex back from it before I reflect it, that is, I turn back from it before I can fully identify with it. It is tricky to do and takes a lot of practice and it held me up for many years. I kept saying to myself "I must get resec before I die. It is the only thing worth doing". I struggled unsuccessfully always thinking it a kind of course which if I followed faithfully I would eventually reach the goal. At last I realised to stop trying for the more I tried the more I stopped myself from succeeding. So I stopped trying, and I stopped trying to stop, and I got there, I understood. It came very slowly and I can not say when it started or stopped. The whole process occurred somewhere either side of the two experiences I have already mentioned in my booklets, notably 'The Way', the experience some call ecstasy or rapture. You can say these two experiences were the icing on the cake. And then I realised I had got nowhere. But I was not the same. Something had happened.

10)   *Realisation is just ordinary, nothing special*

This is a peculiarly Taoistic and Zen idea. When a Zen master was asked what Enlightenment was he replied "Nothing special. When you are hungry eat, when you sit sit, when you stand stand, when you walk walk, Above all don`t wobble." So I realised there was no goal to be reached. After all, what would I do if I reached the goal ? What was left ? Only boredom ? I once wrote in a booklet "What is the meaning of life" I replied "Life has no meaning: life is full of meaning. Meaning is the mean between two statements. If you say Life is relative, is that which is both positive and negative, the meaning is that which lies between them. What lies between them is Life itself. In other words life is all three. Life is two contrary forces plus a third, which is neutral. Yes, it all sounds baffling. Yet once seen it is quite simple. You can read all the books, study as much as you like and never get it. And when you get it you exclaim "Is that it" YES. For there is no goal. Life just is. That is all you need to know Yet that sounds so banal. When you get it that is the explosion Yes, Life just is, but you see it now as pristine, new minted, vibrant and overwhelmingly wonderful. The simple pencil on the desk glows with new life. William Blake said "The fool sees not the same tree the wise man sees." Jesus said "Except ye be as little children ye shall not see the Kingdom". The man or woman who has Realised is a child but a wise child, a fool but a wise fool. The goal, which is no goal, the path, which is no path, is simply the full realisation of life in all its glory, majesty, power and love. In essence Life is Love. The rest is silence.

I hover
As an eagle
Motionless
In boundless space
Outstretched wings
Perfectly balanced
Sublime equilibrium
I am nothing
I am all things
In all eternity
I am alive !

Book 2

SELF–NAUGHTING

For what shall it profit a man, if he shall gain the whole world
and lose his own soul?

Mark 8:36

There sometimes comes a time when one knows and feels, at least in part, what is the essence, meaning and purpose of all life. This knowledge and feeling is at once very complex and yet also very simple. Let us consider this a little.

Why is it complex?

Simply because the world and the individual and all life is complex.

Why is it simple?

Simply because life itself is fundamentally simple.

For life simply is. That, in the last analysis, is all one can say about it.

Here we have the first paradox. As we progress we shall see that everything is a paradox. In fact, when you have truly understood the meaning of paradox then you have understood the mystery of life.

Let us think of the first proposition; life is complex. Clearly, how the world, by which I mean not only our planet but the universe, the entire cosmos, comes about is an immense and aeon-long process. How did it all start? At this present time we think only materially, spiritually never enters the equation. Modern science never considers in depth, simply assumes, the accidental origin of things and starts to study the evolution of the first atoms and amoebae and how they developed into the world we know today, from the primeval swamp and into the Big Bang and so on upwards.

11

However there is another way of studying this procedure. This is by what is called The Ancient Wisdom, an age-old system of knowledge and wisdom hardly known about today. It is also sometimes called The Perennial Philosophy or Wisdom and is the origin and unifier of all the major religions, although they have all, at least in their orthodox and popular aspects, become degraded and only the shreds and dregs of the original teaching remains. But this teaching can still be found in the various texts, writings, scriptures and commentaries of the ancients.

What of the second proposition? That has already been expressed: life simply is. That, in the last analysis, is all one can say about it. Yet when we come to think about it and our place in it we find that in order to fully understand what life is we need to consider what our life is, our own individual life, in relation to universal life.

And so we come to self-naughting.

What does this mean? To what does this refer? Shortly it means dying to self. 'I'm none the wiser,' I hear you say.

Clearly it cannot mean killing oneself in the physical sense. Yet it does mean that in a non-physical sense. Why do it, where is the value? The value is in the greatest possible joy it is possible to experience and is at the same time necessary to fully understand the complexity and meaning of life, its purpose and man's optimum way of life in it.

A human being is, by tradition, a spirit, a soul and a body. He does not have a soul, he is a soul, strung between a spirit and a body. The spirit is the source of all things, the spirit of universal life, and is formless. The body is a material, formed and circumscribed object. This body and spirit starts off as a baby who knows nothing of the world or him or herself. Everything is all one, not yet separated out. As he grows, is given a name, is educated in the mode of his time, he slowly becomes a personality as opposed to an individual (more on this later) and sees himself as a separate being. Survival is the driving force, in humans as it is in all animals. He clings on to his personality, his sense of identity. The average person never considers his soul or spirit. These are the true essence of the being, his true, higher self. He can choose, if he wishes or wills, to identify with his spirit and soul or contrariwise his body.

Normally he does the latter. When the ancient teaching says, as indeed all religions do, one must die to the self, it refers to the lower self, what is normally called the ego, not the higher self, the spiritual. Dying to his body entails losing the only vehicle he has to experience the world.

So it doesn't mean losing his body, his ego, in the physical sense, but in the spiritual and formless sense The soul, strung between spirit and body, can move between the two. If it chooses spirit it becomes immortal, if it chooses body it becomes mortal

'For what shall it profit a man, if he shall gain the whole world, and lose his own soul ?' (Mark 8: 36)

What does it mean to lose one's soul? As already mentioned, the soul is strung between spirit and body. The soul in itself is pure spirit inhabiting a body. As spirit it is in essence identical with the universal spirit, which is God. (My mentor, Eugene Halliday, called this source of all things and phenomena, 'Absolute Sentient Power', ASP for short.) The soul lives in the body for the period of its incarnation. After death it becomes reincarnated in a new body, for the soul is basically immortal. What is normally called the self is the lower self, being what is known as the ego, consisting of the psyche and the material body (the soul is the higher self, the still small voice, the true self). After the death of the material body the psyche lives on for a while and then it, too, dies. (The psyche is the source of the formless aspects of the body, the feelings, passions, loves and hates, pleasures and pains etc.) The psyche is also linked to the consciousness, but the latter is more than the psyche as it is linked to the universal consciousness which is God.

Eugene once said to me, 'I have no ego'. This means he had conquered the ego, i.e. his lower self, and lived fully in his higher self. He had not died, in the physical sense, to his ego, he had simply conquered it: he was

13

now in control of it instead of being controlled by it. He was now the master of himself, not the servant, the slave of the ego. He lived in the spirit, not the body, was identified with the spirit, not the body. (This is not to say the body is not spirit, it is, but on a far lower level. In fact, everything is spirit but on various levels, various vibrations, various modes of being.)

Eugene had found freedom. This is what is meant by becoming a sage, an avatar, a master, a spiritual teacher. He was no longer a separate, isolated being like us, but related to all beings and the universe. He was whole. Thus he served God, not himself.

Very few do this, for the Way, the Path, is hard. Yet in the fullness of time, all must tread it. For The Universal Spirit will not be satisfied until the whole of creation has reached liberation, enlightenment. A tall order! But God has all eternity.

I wrote earlier about personality and individuality. What is the difference?

Personality is from the Latin persona, meaning 'mask' and refers to the mask worn by actors in the ancient Greek drama, and represents the character the actor is playing, the actor himself being in or behind the mask. The mask is the personality of the actor, the actor himself is the individual. One day the actor may play Othello, the next, Hamlet, which being temporary impersonations are not real. Only the actor, the individual, is real. (Individual not divided from the one, the immortal spirit, which is the unity of all life and all beings.) The person is the ego — psyche, lower mind, body — the individual is the soul, the spirit.

The human spirit has two selves, a lower and a higher. Both come from the universal spirit, as does everything else. The lower self is the ego, has form and is mortal; the higher self is pure spirit, is pure consciousness, is formless, and is immortal. If the being identifies with the ego, as it normally does, it lives out its life, dies, is ultimately reborn in a new body and then dies again. It repeats this cycle, hopefully progressing in purity, virtue, and knowledge, until eventually it is able to conquer its ego and lower self, i.e., is no longer a slave to it, and so discovers its higher self, its still small voice, its true self. When it reaches this point, it has found itself. It knows who it is, it can at last say, in full knowledge of its significance, 'I am I', or as the Hindu maxim is, Tat tvam asi (That are thou). The individual self knows itself to be one with, to be identical to, the One Self. This Self is that in which, or in whom, there is no other. The individual is then said to be enlightened. He has reached his term beyond which he cannot go while still living in this physical world. (After this world he can reach to even greater heights.)

To become enlightened is the purpose of life and is the reason behind reincarnation. Although it is possible to experience a sudden illuminative flash and so become enlightened at once, it is so rare that few achieve it. Most need to pass through repeated births to reach the goal. (Hindu tradition says the average is seven lives from the Awakening.) Many people at different periods of their lives experience various stages towards enlightenment which deeply enrich them and give them a definite impulse towards moving more rapidly along the path, for these periods once experienced are never forgotten, for they have given a glimpse of the rewards that lie ahead: joy, peace, harmony, and an absolute certainty of the goodness that rules the universe. All worry and anxiety are gone for ever, only serenity remains. William James called them 'peak experiences', and my mentor, Eugene Halliday, wrote, 'So important is this for human evolution and the attainment of freedom and the power to produce an adequate response to every conceivable situation that if its full import were grasped, the whole effort of humanity would be directed towards its attainment'.

If to work towards this state of enlightenment is so important for the future of humanity, and indeed, for the future existence of the individual, why do so few do it, why is it so little known? Would the average intelligent being prefer to merely live out their allotted span, die, and that's it? To be no more? I think not. Surely, they would rather live on in a state of 'peace that passes all understanding' in harmony with all the world and with all beings, knowing all worry, all anxiety and all fear over for ever! 'Tis a consummation devoutly to be wish'd. (Hamlet)

The reason why so few make the attempt is simple ignorance. We now live in a world where science is the new religion; a materialistic world in which the world of the spirit is barely mentioned. In the West death is a taboo subject and most ordinary people, conditioned by modern education systems, regard death as the end of things and modern medicine is geared to saving life at all costs. Actually death is a natural part of life which has its term and when that term comes, should be allowed to occur without interference.

So the majority of people try to avoid death at all costs, thinking it is the end, and when they die that is it, they will then be no more. When they are young, death is so far distant they never give it a thought, but as they grow older and they begin to realise their own demise as an ever nearer and certain event, they become anxious and fearful. Most are usually more fearful of the manner of their death — will it be long drawn out and fearful? — after they have actually died they will not be there to know and so it will not matter (or so they think). The more this fear and anxiety grows as death approaches, the more the fear develops until it eventually makes the actual death process itself far worse than it should have been. Yet it needn't be like this. If the being prepares him or herself for death it is seen for what it truly is, a transition from one state of being to another. Yes, the physical body dies, but the human being is so much more than the physical body, the being is also soul and spirit, it is actually immortal and never dies. The great Hindu scripture, the Bhagavad Gita, says 'That which is, has always been: that which is not has never been'. So what is there to fear? The new life ultimately is so much better than the one just left.

But, as has been said, to become enlightened is the purpose of life, and very few do this, for even if they may know of it, the Way, the Path, is hard. Christ said that to reach the Kingdom of Heaven (his phrase for Enlightenment or Self-Realisation) one has to tread the Narrow Way.

What is this Narrow Way?

And what is the Broad Way and what the difference between them?

'Enter ye in at the strait gate: for wide is the gate, and broad is the way, that leadeth to destruction, and many there be which go in thereat: Because strait is the gate, and narrow is the way, which leadeth unto life, and few there be that find it.' (Matt 7:13-14)

Eugene has some interesting things to say about this.

'Those who tread the narrow way do so in order to gain the centrality of self-awareness which alone can stop the disintegrating tendencies of life's energies, so that the self, the human soul, can determine from within itself its own life-course.'

Those who meander along the broad way do so in search of pleasurable experiences of any and every kind, not knowing that the search for pleasure spreads out the life energies and disintegrates them, so that no meaningful patterns of life can emerge. The final end of the broad way is total meaninglessness and the dissolution of the self. And just before this final dissolution is experienced the worst of all human conditions, the state of absolute boredom, in which one exists, but has no meaning for one's existence. It is in this state that the soul begins to will its dissolution, its own escape from the pointlessness of a life that has become a non-life, a living death, the only escape from which is self-annihilation.

What a strange piece of dialectic we have here. A man strolls along the broad way, idly seeking and taking whatever pleasures he can find. He believes that life is for pleasure, that life without pleasure would be worthless. He does not notice that his responses to the stimuli that once gave him pleasure are gradually losing interest value. Only when the diminishing returns of his pleasure pursuit become obvious to him, so that he can no longer ignore the un-profit of his life does he finally find himself face to face with his own emptiness.

But the dialectic of the narrow way goes exactly contrary to the broad way. The man who treads the narrow way does so because he believes that before all else he must learn to be himself, to make himself a unity of spirit, soul, mind and body.

And Eugene goes on to further expound this idea. So tread the narrow way, choose the way that makes for more abundant life. As Eugene said the broad way leads to the dispersion of one's energies.

There is the Greek myth of Atalanta, who was a very fast runner, and to keep off her many suitors said she would only marry the one who could beat her in a race. Many tried and failed. At last a wily challenger obtained three golden balls and threw them one by one in front of her, which distracted her and as she stopped to pick them up he got past her and so won, and she became his bride.

So, distraction is the enemy. The way, the narrow way, is the way of the single mind, of one-pointedness, of one's main aim and target, the way, self-realisation, of enlightenment. (See Christian Philosophy Book 2, by Eugene Halliday, pages 56-58.)

There are many ways to going about becoming self-realised, many ways of treading the path of the Narrow Way. Why not just start by simply putting your first foot on the path? 'Journey of a thousand miles begins with the first step', says Lao Tzu. Start by just preferring the Narrow Way to the Broad Way. By just making this simple act of preference you will have taken the first step along the path. That first act of will, provided it is a true and honest act, will put you in tune and touch, in resonance with your true self, your higher self, which is at one with the greater Self, who is the sole creator of all things and all phenomena. The Narrow Way and the Broad Way are opposites. The choice is one or the other, wholeness or separation.

'No man can serve two masters: for either he will hate the one, and love the other: or else he will hold to the one, and despise the other. Ye cannot serve God and Mammon' (Matt. 6: 24).

Once made, the decision to prefer the former, and you are on the Narrow Way. The goal is now certain and you will begin to see results, for the Self, who knows all things, will start to help you. He will work through his instrument which is your higher, true self, your still small voice, which can only be heard when the normal clatter and busy-busy cacophony of the mind is stilled. The computer, which is the lower mind, must be switched off before 'The Voice of the Silence' can be heard. This voice is always right and will give good advice, which should be thought through carefully and then acted upon. (But be sure it is not your normal voice trying to fool you, for the capacity for self-deceit is infinite. Your lower mind will fight to the death to maintain the status quo and go back to its normal selfish ways.) But if your will is pure and firm you will always know when the silent voice is speaking. Also, odd things will start to happen. Jung called these strange coincidences synchronicities. In the street, bus or train, at the supermarket, anywhere in fact, you will suddenly meet an old acquaintance you hadn't seen for years who will suggest a particular book he is reading, or will put you in touch with a great friend of his, a very wise man, who can help you. You will begin to wonder if some strange benevolent power is not helping you. Believe me, there is (I speak from experience).

This power is God, a little word that people are wary of in these materialistic days, but who in reality is the supreme power that is the source and origin of all things, and knows and helps any being who is beginning to sense His presence, and so is beginning to realise the true aim of all beings is to return to his true home, back to his Father's house, where is the only peace and harmony, joy and bliss, which everybody is unconsciously seeking and yet does not know how to get.

To start with, don't alter your life in any way, for you will not yet have the ability to do so. Except, and this is important, keep firm in your resolve to prefer the Narrow Way to the Broad Way. You may find your life subtly and slowly changing. This is because you have made a change of will, and the will, which is the only power which can initiate change, is now working in harmony with the great Will which has created the universe, and so is now working in tune with you. Thus your aim is now assured. However long it takes you cannot fail. What greater security can you have? With it you are already relieved of the fear and anxiety that the majority of people suffer from. And you have only just begun the journey! Simply preferring the one Way to the other. 'No man can serve two masters: for either he will hate the one and love the other, or else he will hold to the one and despise the other. Ye cannot serve God and Mammon.' In my booklets, I always referred to the Nothing and the Something, which are the Narrow and the Broad Way respectively.

At the beginning of this piece I referred to the paradox being behind everything. Life is a Duality yet also Unity. The Nothing (Narrow Way) is God, the Supreme Spirit, the origin of all things and phenomena which is formless and invisible, and yet is in all things. It is the Life and essence in all things. 'And God breathed into all things the Spirit of Life and Man became a living Soul.' The Something (Broad Way) is the visible and manifested universe, the circumscribed form, which can be said to be the body of God, just as the flesh can be said to be the body of Man. This is the first paradox, for God is one who has become two, the nothing who has become something, the formless who has become formed. There are actually two paradoxes here. The first is the unity, the formless becoming formed while still remaining formless, as just described; the second is the universe itself, which is a unity, yet is also a duality, for it consists of both the formless invisible essence, the soul of the universe which is the Spirit of God, and the formed and visible body which is the manifestation.

Thus God is a paradox, being both Himself and His body the universe.

Thus the universe is a paradox, being both spirit and flesh, formless and formed.

Man is also a paradox, being both consciousness and body.

Everywhere is paradox. Everywhere is the Nothing and the Something. And the Nothing is the Something and the Something is the

Nothing. All is not one, yet not two, as the Sanscrit Advaita says.

This all seems to be very confusing and hard to grasp. This is because it is the most difficult concept to explain and yet is the secret of all meaning. Perhaps a simpler way of explanation is to say that the origin of all things is the Nothing, which is a no-thing, and yet contains all things within it, as a seed which grows beneath the ground and then bursts up and out into the sunlight as a flower, or as an egg which bursts out of the bird and breaks, and the new bird appears as a new life, while the mother bird still lives. In the east, the main symbol of life is the lotus, which grows deep in the mud at the bottom of the pool, climbs up through the water, budding through the surface into that wondrous flower, which has its root in the mud, its stem in the water, and its flower floating on the surface in the sunlight. Or again, to the ancient Greeks, the symbol of life was that apparently inexplicable metamorphosis or transformation of the caterpillar through the cocoon to the butterfly. (The Greek word for butterfly and the soul is psyche.) Or even shorter and less poetic — the Nothing, while remaining itself and the intelligent Spirit, contains the Something within it as its mode of being and action.

Samsara is Nirvana and vice versa according to Hindu and Buddhist philosophy. This is another way of saying the same thing. Samsara is the world of things and all phenomena, is the world of the ego, the small self; Nirvana is not complete annihilation as is commonly supposed in the west, but is the supreme spirit and cause of the world, the big Self. Samsara is the Something, the formed; Nirvana is the Nothing, the formless. The Nothing produces the Something; the Something does not produce the Something.

But what has all this to do with self-naughting? Well, we as beings, are both the nothing and the something, for we have come out of the nothing and are now the something. We are dual, for we are spirit and body, and yet we are one. We are an exact replica of the universe, a microcosm of the macrocosm. As spirit we are a tiny spark sent forth from the fire that is the Supreme Intelligent Spirit; as body we are the manifestation, the material form of that Spirit. We are the tiny spiritual soul in that body in order for the

Spirit, which never forget is an Intelligent Spirit, to have an infinite number of souls with which to experience the myriad possibilities of life, to enrich and enlarge life. That mysterious thing we call Life is that very Intelligent Spirit we call God, Allah, Brahman, Tao etc., experimenting with itself, playing with itself, creating with itself, in order to discover and bring forth into manifestation its potential possibilities. We are as intelligent cells in the body of that Spirit, just as our own bodies are composed of intelligent cells cooperating, when healthy, to create a harmonious system.

So why this need for self-naughting? As already mentioned several times, we are, so to speak, two existences in one, for we are a spiritual immortal soul, and we are a physical mortal body called the ego. We are of the whole and we are of the separate self. As the whole we are of the Supreme Spirit, and as the separate self we are of the Part. This is therefore the problem. We can either serve the whole or serve just our selves. We are either selfless or selfish.

By thinking of our self as a separate being in a world of other separate beings we cause all the troubles of the world. Our primary purpose being survival, we are naturally wary of the other beings interfering with that survival, and so are ready to fight if necessary to safeguard it. Thus disharmony, not harmony. By thinking of our self as a separate part of a whole, we are fully in tune and resonance with total reality. Thus harmony, not disharmony. We are not merely separate drops in the ocean of life, but separate drops knowing we owe our existence to the indisputable fact of there being an ocean of life. Without the ocean of life, no life; without which we would not exist at all. So, when we realise this, we have a choice, either to continue living our lives as a separate being, living just for our own pleasure and thus as a selfish being, or to change our way of life so that we become, to use Christ's word, reborn, and thus to continue life as before but with the addition of living not only for our selves, but also for the whole, for the world. We work for the world as well as for ourselves. We become selfless, not selfish.

Surely, understanding this, the choice is obvious. The normal, honest, decent person would choose to work for the whole world, not just for oneself. But actually, of course, when one tries to help the world one is also helping oneself at the same time.

One has now committed oneself to walking the Narrow Way and not the Broad Way. And this is where the problem begins. To walk the Narrow Way is hard. It may take a short time or it may take a lifetime. It may, probably will, take many. But no matter. Once you are on the path you will, if you are a normal, decent human being, never look back. (Remember Lot`s wife, remember Orpheus. Both looked back. Lot's wife was turned to a pillar of salt, Orpheus lost his beloved Eurydice.) But if you keep going and don't falter, even if you just prefer to tread that path but don't yet feel you are able to (though remember St. Augustine's early plea, 'Dear God, make me perfect but not yet'), just that preferring is sufficient.

You will find your life subtly changing for the better. You will become calmer, your anxieties will begin to cease, life in general will start to look up. At first you will not notice any change, but slowly, imperceptibly, it will creep up on you and become stronger as the days wear on, until finally you will realise with absolute certainty that there is some unknown and benevolent power silently helping you on your path — which path is, to align yourself with its purposes.

You, from henceforth, will be working for the universal spirit, not your own spirit. But because you are, in your own essential spirit, part of that universal spirit, you are, in working for it, also working for yourself.

This is what makes for the harmony, peace and love for all humanity and all forms of life, that you now find in yourself. All anxieties, depressions, and fears are gone for ever. ''Tis a consummation devoutly to be wish'd.' But, as already stated, the way is hard. Yet once the choice has been made the path gets easier. 'The choice', the initial choice, yes, that is the most difficult bit of all. For it involves the Will. We have two choices in all matters, either to choose this or that, one or the other. (It is no use refusing to choose, for that is itself a choice, for it is saying, 'I choose to refuse to choose'.) As Christ says, it is either God or Mammon. You must choose one or the other. (If you refuse to choose, then you have in effect chosen neither life or death, but only voidity, non existence. There will then be no chance of living in bliss and harmony or living and enjoying all the pleasures and pains of the world. You will not be moving upwards or downwards. Thus your non-choice will have become the choice of pure nihilism.) So choose self-naughting. Choose Life, choose Freedom, choose Love.

'For what shall it profit a man if he shall gain the whole world and lose his own soul?'

Book 3

THE YOUNG MAN AND THE OLD MAN

A DIALOGUE

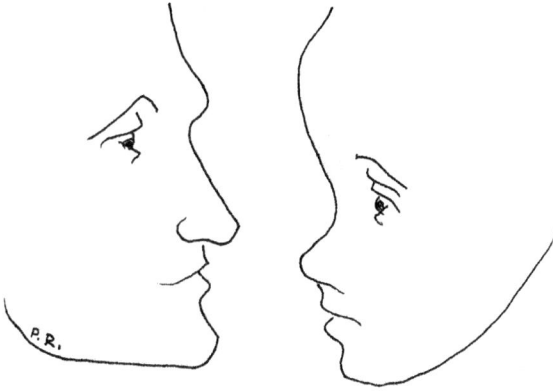

'Old age' said the young man,
His mouth full of teeth,
'Is an empty cave
On a desolate heath',

'Nothing left to bite on,
To crunch a dainty sweet:
Only toothless gums
To suck a mother's teat'.

'Old age' said the grown man,
A gap or two showing,
'Is an empty cave
Where a treasure is growing',
'Nothing left to bite on,
Memory is let loose:

Only when the teeth are gone
Do you suck the juice'.

'Old age' said the old man,
From a mouth all bare,
'Is an empty cave
At the foot of the stair',

'When the cave is full,
Eating takes your time:
When all that's left is hollow.
Then you begin to climb.

Young Man   Sir, may I ask you a question?

Old Man   Surely.

YM   Am I right in thinking you have never been to a university?

OM   Yes that is so.

YM   Well, I did and I have a BSc and a BA to prove it.

OM   So?

YM   What I don't understand is you talk logically and sensibly about so
       many things. You mention names I have never heard of, you use
       ideas and concepts entirely new to me. I was taught nothing of
       this at university. How did you come by it, from where did you get
       your knowledge? Is not the university the place that holds the core
       of knowledge?

OM   Knowledge of the word, yes. My knowledge goes beyond the world, yet still includes it.

YM   I'm not sure I understand. What do you mean, 'goes beyond the world'?

OM   There are many worlds. But for our present purposes there are two: this visible world we see all around us and another invisible world behind it, which in fact, gives rise to this visible world. Unless we know and understand this invisible world we can never understand the visible one.

YM   'This invisible world'. Do you mean the world of religion? The kingdom of heaven — and hell — and all that?

OM   Yes, in a way. But orthodox religion — how can I say — orthodox religion distorts the teaching, the truth, in certain ways. What you learn at university is usually this version, and so you never come to realise the basic truths. These are the truths I speak of.

YM   Then where do I find those?

OM   They are found in all the ancient scriptures, teachings and traditions. In the Hindu Vedanta and Buddhism, the Bhagavad Gita, the Persian Zoroastrian, the Chinese Tao, the Egyptian Hermetic and the Judaic, which includes the Christian and the Islamic.

YM   I know a little of the Christian but almost nothing of the others.
OM   They are all saying the same thing but in different languages and in terms of the understanding of their respective cultures. There is only one truth and it has always been known.
YM   Then why don't we know it? Why isn't it taught in the university?

OM   Jesus said, 'Look under a stone, I am there. Split a block of wood, you will find me'. He also said, 'The Kingdom of Heaven is spread throughout the world and men do not see it'.

YM   Isn't that Pantheism?

OM   No, not properly understood. The truth is not hidden, it is everywhere if you know how to look. It is in your own heart.

YM   Then how do you look?

OM   Another thing Jesus said was, 'Except ye repent ye shall not see the Kingdom of Heaven'. What does repent mean?

YM   To be sorry for what you have done. To realise you have sinned and to sin no more.

OM   What does sin mean?

YM   It means to do wrong, to be, in some sort, kind of — evil.

OM   The orthodox church translates these two words, repent and sin, in a misleading way, a moralistic way. They actually have a precise and technical meaning. Repent means to rethink, as in 'to rethink one's position'. It can apply in any situation. Being sorry for what you have done needn't necessarily come into it. You may not be sorry but decide to repent, to 'rethink', simply because it's more efficient in your present circumstances. And sin actually means 'to miss the mark', as in archery. You have only been wrong in that you haven't hit the target, achieved your aim, whatever that aim may be. You see how the church puts a moralistic gloss on the words and thus instills a guilt in you.

YM   Why does t he church do that?

OM   For its own purposes. To maintain its power. The church says the only way to be forgiven for your sins and taught how to repent, is to accept the teachings of the Holy Fathers, the self proclaimed ambassadors of God.

Another teaching of Christ is that you must be reborn. This is another way of saying 'repent'. The Greek word is metanoia which as well as meaning 'rethink' also carries the connotation of 'turn around', as is someone facing South who turns around to face North. Note the precision of the Greek, for it has the idea not just of any old rethinking, which may be as inefficient as the original thinking, but a complete 180 degree turn right round to the opposite viewpoint.

YM   So you are saying you must see everything from the opposite point of view to that which is generally accepted?

OM   Yes. Although without denying that general view.

YM   But wouldn't that put you at odds with society? You would be regarded as completely out of phase with life. You would be thought crazy.

OM   Yes, you usually are. True seekers after truth have a hard time of it. But you are not out of phase with life, it is normal folk who are out of phase with life. The truth, the reality, embraces both points of view. I am referring to a total and holistic view of reality, normal society has a partial view.

YM   Now we are back where we started. What is this total view?

OM   The total view sees life, creation, reality, God — call it what you will — as one, a simple unity. This is not Pantheism, for Pantheism says everything is God and that is all there is, that Nature is God. This is true up to a point, for Nature is God, yet God is also beyond Nature.

YM   I don't understand.

OM   Put it like this. First, there is an unformed 'somewhat'. It has no
      name for it is prior to the naming process. This somewhat is all
      there is, there is nothing else. This somewhat is aware of itself. It is
      intelligent. And it is all alone. The human mind cannot
      comprehend the true essence of this somewhat, how it is to itself.
      It is eternal, infinite, it was never born, it will never die, it is the
      source of all things, past, present and to come. We have to name
      something before we can come to terms with it, so Christians call
      it God, Muslims Allah, the Chinese, Tao, the Hindus Brahman,
      and so on. But these names mean nothing. They say nothing
      about the essence of ultimate reality.

YM   How then can we know anything about it?

OM   Because the 'somewhat', God, comes into the world so we can see
      Him. He manifests himself. The invisible incomprehensibility
      emanates down into a visible comprehensibility. The universe is
      created, which we can see and touch and wonder at.

YM   Is the universe then God's body?

OM   Yes, you can say that. It's rather similar to you being your body,
      yet feeling and knowing in your consciousness that you are also
      more than your body. It is actually very simple, yet at the same
      time a difficult concept for a modern mind to grasp, for modern
      education teaches a completely false picture of the true actuality.
      The Church is mainly responsible for this, for it teaches that there
      is a God, a Supreme Being, who creates a world which is yet
      separate from him. There is God, and there is the Creation. Two
      separate entities. The ancients say something different. They say
      the two are one, that God is in everything, there is nothing
      anywhere that is not God. As you say, you can consider the
      universe to be God's body. God in Himself is his consciousness of
      that body, just as you have a body and a consciousness of that
      body which is yet more than that body. Once you see this it opens

up a totally different view of ultimate reality from that of the church.

YM   How did you come to know all this?

OM   I was taught by a man incomparably greater than myself. That is how it is normally passed down, from person to person, from teacher to teacher. It is extremely rare for an individual to find out himself, unless it comes to him directly in some sort of vision from the Supreme Spirit himself. There is a saying, 'When the pupil is ready the master will appear'. And as the rabbis say, 'Men eat fruit from trees planted by men they never knew'. Jesus said, 'Seek and ye shall find, knock and it shall be opened'. Anyone who earnestly seeks to know the truth will find doors opening apparently miraculously in all directions. The opportunity will be offered to him. All he has to do is take it. Many don't, they give up at the first hurdle.

YM   Why is that'?

OM   The way is hard, and requires certain conditions. Most people are not prepared to accept them.

YM   What are these conditions?

OM   First you must be earnest and completely sincere in your seeking the truth. You must be prepared to give up things, make sacrifices, for what you seek is the greatest gift the world can offer. The Supreme Spirit offers you a choice. The choice is there for all men and women, and they have to choose one way or the other, whether they will or no. Even if, out of ignorance, they refuse to choose, it is as if they have chosen 'No'. The choice is always there, waiting, and one is left entirely free to choose, no one forces anyone.

YM   And the choice is?

31

OM   To give yourself up to God, to elect to be – so to speak – His steward in the world, His ambassador, and working for His purposes. Or to live as most people do, for themselves, a separate individual in a world of other individuals all striving to maintain and better themselves and survive in what they see as a hostile world.

YM   H'm. That needs thinking about.

OM   Let me expand on this a bit. To work for God or to work for yourself, that is the choice. Even if you are not aware of it. Yet everyone knows deep in their innermost core, deep in their heart. You can make this choice any time. And even if you don't think you have the courage, you can choose to prefer to serve God than serve yourself. Actually, of course, you serve both at the same time. Just making that preference will change everything. You will feel a strange power coming into you, very faint at first, yet growing increasingly stronger. This power is on your side. It will not let you down. You can trust it utterly. That power is God, is Love, is your own inner and deeper true self of which you are normally not conscious, coming to the surface and beginning to take over your life. That power knows better than you how to act in your everyday life, and it will protect you and tell you what to do in whatever circumstance comes upon you. That power is God acting in the place in which you are. You will be hearing your own 'still small voice', which is God. Listen to it. That is metanoia. You will be reborn and will have turned your life around. You will see the world anew, all anxieties will fall away, you will be as a new born babe.

YM   That sounds marvellous. Why doesn't everyone do it?

OM   From fear. It takes courage. You have to take a leap in the dark, leap over the precipice, and trust that the Supreme Spirit will protect you. He will. But how do you know that until you actually do it. And the actual doing of it is an act of will. You have to turn your will around. That is the metanoia. That takes courage. Yet the Spirit makes it easy for you.

YM   How?

OM   You don't need, of course, to actually leap over any precipice, that is just a figure of speech. But the equivalent to the leap, the sudden conversion, is very rare. A few people, without any apparent warning, in a flash turn their whole lives around. But for most people, just preferring to choose 'to fight the good fight' sets them on the straight and narrow path, which grows increasingly easy the further one travels. As Lao Tse said, 'A journey of a thousand miles begins with the first step'. Though, paradoxically, the path grows harder, for you meet more and more difficulties in the way of tests of your ability to cope with them. Yet your increasing strength enables you to master them. You also find your love for the whole human race and all creatures becoming all pervasive, and all fear will leave you. 'Perfect love casts out fear.' All you have to do is try it. You won't be disappointed.

YM   But won't you lose yourself if you surrender yourself to Love, as you call it? You will have no will of your own. You will be a —— a nothing.

OM   You will have shed your old self as a snake sheds its skin, and you will be reborn a new self, greater than before. The caterpillar becomes a beautiful butterfly. You will be fulfilling your true purpose in the world.

YM   If doing this is so rare and so few people attempt it then what happens to them?

OM   The Supreme Spirit's purpose is that everything in the universe will ultimately come to this point.

YM   But that will take probably thousands, no, millions of years.

33

OM   Yes it will, no doubt millions. But He is in no hurry, He has all eternity. And as far as the human race is concerned there is no guarantee. As everyone has a choice maybe they will choose to carry on as they are, which will eventually lead to them destroying themselves. But the Spirit will then just produce another more suitable life form that will prove more worthy.

YM   You said all is God, so does He then produce this form out of Himself?

OM   Of course. What the Infinite Spirit is doing is manifesting himself to himself, making actual his own potentiality. In himself he is formless, invisible in the sense we understand the word: he becomes a myriad of forms and is in those forms. Yet at the same time he is not those forms, for in himself he utterly transcends them.

YM   It sounds very mysterious to me. Why he does all this, I mean.

OM   Yes, it is. The universe is a great mystery.

YM   I was taught science at university. You have made no mention of science. Isn't science attempting to solve the mystery?

OM   Yes and no. However it is going about it in the wrong way. It requires empirical proof: every hypothesis and theory has to be tested in the laboratory and it is therefore continually updating its results. Science primarily deals with the material world and tends to ignore the immaterial world, which is ultimately the cause of the material world. But its researches are bringing it ever closer to the truth. The uncertainty principle, the string theory, quantum physics, are all bringing science to the realisation that ultimate reality is not physical but — can I use an unpopular word? — spiritual. In fact, ultimate reality, is, theologically speaking, The Mind of God, or philosophically speaking, Consciousness. Just like your own consciousness. Yes, the universe is a great mystery. And in the last analysis it is beyond the human mind to grasp it. 'Grasp it.' Why did I use that word? For the one thing you cannot do is grasp it, any more than you can grasp water. You cannot really speak of it at all. The Taoist saying is 'Those who speak don't know, those who know don't speak'. The one subject that science should be concentrating on above all else, and which it largely ignores, is the human mind. That is where the answer is found. 'Man, know thyself' says the Delphic oracle. That has been the teaching of all ages.

To sum up, no one knows where or why it all came from, all one can say is that there is an infinite spirit that is Love, and that He produces the world out of himself in order to find Himself — and as a game to play. And He joys and glories in the wonder He finds in Himself. We come from Him, and are in Him and part of Him, so we should do the same. We then find the peace that passes understanding.

The rest is silence.

Book 4

SOME REFLECTIONS ON SACRIFICE

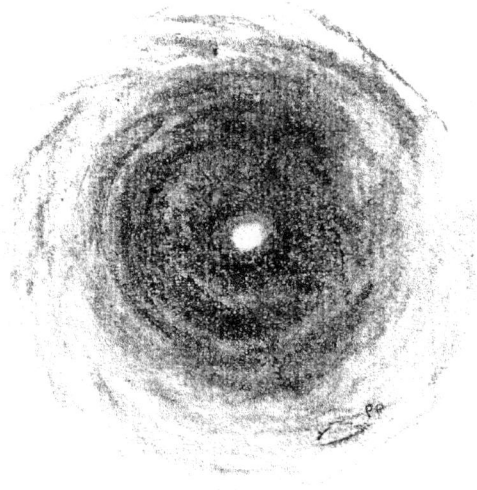

'Take up your cross daily and follow me.'

Christ

Sacrifice is the first Law of Life. What does this mean? What actually is sacrifice? And why is it the first law of life? The word is from the Latin sacer holy, and facere to make; thus 'to make holy'.

Over the centuries it has gradually shifted its meaning, moving from 'and offering to God' to 'killing a victim to appease God' to 'giving up something of value' to 'giving up something of value to gain a greater value' to finally 'a felt sense of loss of something. All these notions contain the idea of giving up something.

Why is it the first Law of Life?

Simply because the first one to give up something was God Himself. And what did He give up?

Himself. God Himself became the first sacrifice when He sacrificed Himself to Himself. ('I am the eater and the eaten' – Samson's riddle in the Bible.) God made an offering of Himself to God – which was Himself.

What does this mean?

God is the term, among many others, used to describe the ultimate sentient intelligent power that is the source of all we know as reality. God is the source of all phenomena, all visibles and all invisibles. There is nothing in the whole of creation and beyond that is not God.

But God is not a being as such. In the sense in which we normally use the term, he does not exist. Existence implies circumscription, and God is not circumscribed. Yet somehow He 'is'. God is formless, a no-thing who yet makes all things. God, who is infinite and totally beyond all circumscription, yet makes the finite, the circumscribed, the universe.

How does He do this?

As there is nothing anywhere that is not Him, as He is all there is, then He must make the universe out of Himself, for there is no other.

And this is the first sacrifice.

Sacrifice is the first Law of Life. What does this mean? What actually is sacrifice? And why is it the first law of life? The word is from the Latin sacer holy, and facere to make; thus 'to make holy'.

Over the centuries it has gradually shifted its meaning, moving from 'and offering to God' to 'killing a victim to appease God' to 'giving up something of value' to 'giving up something of value to gain a greater value' to finally 'a felt sense of loss of something. All these notions contain the idea of giving up something.

Why is it the first Law of Life?

Simply because the first one to give up something was God Himself. And what did He give up? Himself. God Himself became the first sacrifice when He sacrificed Himself to Himself. ('I am the eater and the eaten' – Samson's riddle in the Bible.) God made an offering of Himself to God – which was Himself.

What does this mean?

God is the term, among many others, used to describe the ultimate sentient intelligent power that is the source of all we know as reality. God is the source of all phenomena, all visibles and all invisibles. There is nothing in the whole of creation and beyond that is not God.

But God is not a being as such. In the sense in which we normally use the term, he does not exist. Existence implies circumscription, and God is not circumscribed. Yet somehow He 'is'. God is formless, a no-thing who yet makes all things. God, who is infinite and totally beyond all circumscription, yet makes the finite, the circumscribed, the universe.

How does He do this?

As there is nothing anywhere that is not Him, as He is all there is, then He must make the universe out of Himself, for there is no other.

And this is the first sacrifice.

To circumscribe is to bind, to enclose, to put a circle round that which is free in order to manifest it, to cut it off from the infinite and invisible in order to make it finite and visible. God as such is an infinite invisible power; the universe is a finite visible entity.

God binds Himself in order to exist. He opposes Himself with Himself in order to feel Himself, to see Himself, to manifest Himself to Himself. The universe is the mirror in which He sees His own reflection – reflexion. (These two words mean the same, while having slightly different, but highly important, connotations.)

38

Sit quietly in a chair and gradually allow yourself to totally relax. After a while you feel your integument beginning to spread out into your surroundings so you are no longer conscious of your body as a separate entity. You feel yourself becoming, how can one say? amorphous. Now suddenly press one closed fist into the other open palm quite hard. Immediately there is resistance and the amorphous feeling has gone. Something has come to 'be', there is 'something there' that wasn't before. If you press really hard there is the beginning of pain. There is now a sense of the loss of the previous undifferentiated feeling and a gaining of a more sharply focussed feeling.

Something has come to be that wasn't there before. Yet a price has to be paid. Think of the air all around us. It is free, expansive, nothing constrains it, and nothing can be done with it. Now take some air and constrain it, circumscribe it by confining it in a container. It is now a force that can be used. But the price is the loss of its freedom.

God is a free spirit. To make the world, which is His body, He must sacrifice His freedom.

Some would call this Pantheism, for pantheism says, 'God is all there is, and all is God'. This implies that God can only be found it nature, in the creation. But God, as an infinite free spirit, is the creation and at the same time transcends the creation.
 When the infinite intelligent spirit creates the universe, a duality is created. God is both the creation and that which is beyond the creation. Draw a circle and you at once both include and exclude. No matter how large your circle you cannot include that which will always lie beyond it. This duality, this two-fold aspect of the one reality, is the Second Law of Life, namely the Law of Polarity.

God, an intelligent free spirit, crucifies Himself in order to manifest, in order to, as we would say, 'Exist'. He hangs Himself on a cross, for a cross is the intersecting of two forces. The vertical arm is the free initiating power thrusting down and acting upon the horizontal arm, which is the inert substance of the universe, and vivifying it. They are both aspects of the one sentient power in its two modes of behaviour, and each needs the other.

You can feel this in yourself. Sit in a chair again and think about yourself and who you are. Firstly, you are a body, which you can think of as your own tiny universe, and which you can see and touch. Then, secondly, you have an awareness of your body. But can you see and touch this awareness? No one has ever seen 'awareness'. And yet, in truth, this awareness is more real than the reality of your body. In fact, without it you wouldn't even know you had a body.

You are a free spirit in a circumscribed body. We are all sacrifices. In order to exist we have consciously given up certain aspects of our freedom. Yet the free spirit is still there hidden in our body, although for the most part, we don't realise it.

In the centre of a tropical storm there is the 'eye of the storm', a totally calm area between the anti-clockwise winds first blowing in, and then blowing out. (Northern hemisphere.) This eye-of-the-storm is your inner voice, your own still calm centre, the voice of your God silently speaking directly to you. It is, in essence, identical with the free spirit outside the whirling rotation of turbulence. These two are the 'Immanent Spirit' and the 'Transcendent Spirit' of theological doctrine.

(If you have ever actually been in a real 'eye of the storm' out at sea, it is the strangest and, let's face it, the most frightening experience. One minute your tiny vessel is being buffeted about by tremendous seas and hurricane force winds such that you think your last hour has come. Then without warning, in a matter of seconds, the wind totally ceases and the huge seas, now bereft of wind to give them direction, rise up all at once from every point of the compass like a million angry hydras. You are now in the eye. You remain in this quite weird total calm and eerie silence for perhaps fifteen minutes or half an hour. Then, once more without any warning, the wind suddenly roars up with its old fury but from the completely opposite direction and then, if the Lord looks on you with favour, and you know and obey the rules of tropical storms and you and your vessel are still in one piece, you may reach the safety of the outer world again. For no ordinary man may live for long in the eye.)

The ancients knew all about making an offering to God. For thousands of years they sacrificed their earthly God, the king, in a replication of God's self-sacrifice. It was recognised that in order for there to be a birth there first must be a death. In order for there to be creation God has to sacrifice part of His freedom. Neither can function without the other.

So the ruler, who was the representative of God on earth, had to die in a yearly ritual before being born again. 'The king is dead, long live the king!' This yearly ritual also plays out the yearly death in winter of the sun and all agriculture and the subsequent rebirth in the spring of the sun and new life.

(An interesting sidelight on this is the idea, currently gaining new ground, that the agricultural seasons are related to the axial tilting and the precession of the equinoxes. The idea is that the cataclysm which caused the universal deluge, the Noetic flood of the Bible, which occurred about 11,500 BC, was brought about by a polar shift which tilted the previously vertical axis to its present angle of 23 and a half degrees. This shift caused the seasons and the consequent rise of agriculture. Previously there was a Golden Age in which the climate was equable, there was no seasonal variation and all was peace and harmony. When the polar, axial, tilt occurred precession began, conflict, seasonal variation was the norm, and many new evolutes were brought into being which were not possible under the previous even and equable regime. Jacob Boehme, the 16th century German cobbler and mystic, wrote 'God knew that Adam would eat of the Tree of the Knowledge of Good and Evil'. In other words, it was necessary that the Golden Age of innocence had to end in order for there to be further development and evolution. An interesting thought that's worth considering.)

Eventually this sacred ritual degenerated to the extent that the actual king was not physically killed, but a condemned man, or sometimes even a volunteer, was selected and feted as a 'fool's king' for a year and then ceremonially executed. After a lengthy period even this was changed and an animal killed. The traditional scapegoat, initially an actual physical goat, had arrived.

Abraham was required to sacrifice his son Isaac. Notwithstanding this event showing Abraham's willingness to obey his God absolutely, it may also mark the cross over point from human to animal, as at the last moment a ram was substituted in Isaac's stead. (This myth also has other significances. Why a ram, for instance? Does it mark the onset of the 2,000 year Age of Aries, the age of the ram, due to the precession of the equinoxes?)

Be that as it may, this degeneration entailed a gradual loss of direct communication with the creator. There was no longer a one for one correspondence between God and man. So eventually arose human sacrifice in a ghastly replay of Abraham's earlier required sacrifice, though this time on an immensely larger scale.

The life of a being was held to be linked to the blood. When the blood ran out the person died. The blood was the material and psychic carrier of the soul, which at death passed back into the invisible world of God, the free spirit. So to maintain contact with God many victims were sacrificed and their blood spilt and still living hearts torn out, as it was thought that as they passed into the other world and yet were still, at least for a short period, bound to this one, they could act as a conduit between the two and pass valuable information back to the executing priests. Thousands of victims died in this way. Many actually volunteered, believing they were doing society a service.

Degeneration indeed!

The greatest sacrifice, of course, is that of Jesus Christ. He made Himself into the most significant scapegoat of all time. He followed out in precise detail all the old traditional rituals, and at the same time became the actual God sacrificing Himself for the sake of the world. More that that, He said, Take up your cross daily and follow me. He reminded a decadent and corrupt world that in order to obtain salvation and ultimate reunion with their God, who created the world, then they must do as He does and sacrifice themselves, that is their separate egoic identities, in order to reunite themselves with the free immortal spirit from which they came and which is their true home. Jesus said, Repent. Except ye be born again ye shall not see the kingdom of heaven. 'Repent' simply means 'to rethink'.

Jesus also said, The kingdom of heaven is within you, referring, of course, to the silent inner voice, the still small centre, which is the free spirit, the eye of the storm, at the centre of our being. To reach salvation and enlightenment we must identify with this identify with this inner centre, and to do this we must first die to our lower self, our selfish ego, our material body.

We do not have to kill it, just control it so it does not control us. This is a most difficult task, for the temptations of bodily delights are many and varied. In fact, infinite.

But this is the sacrifice (we) each of us has to make.

Actually, our sacrifice is the exact opposite to God's. Whereas God came down from His pre-creational free-spirit state and limited Himself by circumscribing Himself, we need to move up from our circumscribed mode to the free pre-creational state. As the Hermetic maxim has it – God became Man in order that Man may become God.

The polarity of the two processes, the initiating free, and the subsequent domed, or bound, occur simultaneously. They interpenetrate each other. This is the state in which the great sages, **avatars, rishis,** yogis and saints live. It is a transcendent state of total bliss that includes both good and evil, for they are seen to be the two sides of the golden coin that is the creative life. Joy and sorrow both exist, but are seen to be what they truly are. The world stays the same as before, but is experienced from a completely new viewpoint.

In this world, every light casts a shadow, with one exception. When the sun is directly overhead there is no single point of light cast and so no shadow. The light is evenly spread everywhere. This is bliss. This is enlightenment. In this state we live in the world and experience all its wonders and joys, and at the same time continually remember our origin and the source from which we came.

Eugene Halliday said, Heaven is equilibrated Power.

Book 5

THOUGHTS ON FREEDOM

At any moment you are either
Growing into inertia or freedom.

Eugene Halliday

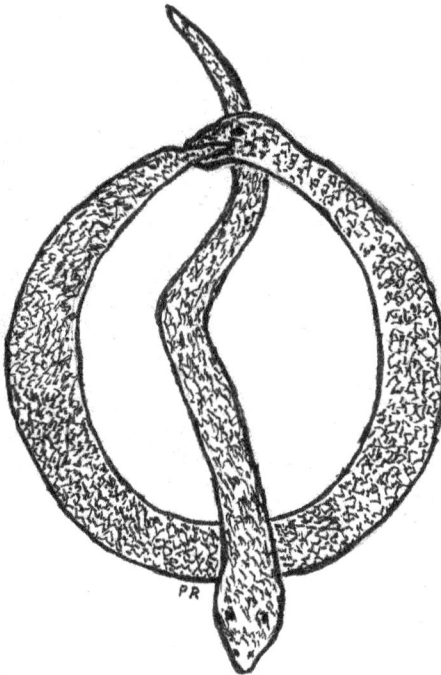

Freedom is one of the most used and also the most abused words in the language. Everybody wants freedom. Men rush madly about killing in the name of freedom, thus denying their victims the very thing they themselves seek. Then they say 'I am free, I can do what I want'. But does this make them free? If you are free to do what you want, that implies a lack, for you still want something. But to be truly free surely means you don`t want anything for you already have it, or else you don`t want it.

So what exactly is freedom?

My version of the first poem of Lao Tzu`s Tao Te King goes like this :--

> The Way of Freedom is never tolled.
> The Names of Freedom are never told.
> Power, the Pa of Matter is free,
> Matter, the Ma of all Forms is bound.
> Pa causes the effects, Ma affects the causes.
> Separately they are not the same,
> Together they make freedom.
> How can one speak of them?
> They are not free,
> They are not doomed,
> They are a free dome.

Here then is perhaps a clue. Freedom — Free-dome. Something that is free while at the same time not free, i.e. domed. Eugene says, 'Freedom is having the ability to choose your own bondage'. To choose your bondage. Most people are bound but do not choose, their bondage being thrust upon them. Bondage you must have. Everybody is bound in at least one aspect, in fact the most significant aspect, for they are free spirits imprisoned in physical bodies. And this is the answer to the clue, for freedom, true freedom that is, is the balance between being free, in the sense of being totally unconstrained, and being partially constrained. A helpful image is to think of a circle. A circle includes and excludes. That within is bound, that without is free. That within, by virtue of its constrainment, as for instance hot water (steam) in a boiler, can drive a locomotive. It can act, do something. That without is free and by virtue of its freeness does nothing, it merely stays where it is, motionless, or else passes through space indefinitely creating nothing. The ancients symbolised these two states as a serpent running free and a serpent with its tail in its mouth. The one snake in its two aspects.

To be useful, to create, the power must meet some obstruction, some resistance, in order to feel itself, in order to be. Hence the creation, hence the universe, hence the individual, hence the free spirit imprisoned in a physical body. Every creation consists of a free essence constrained in a container, that is a form of some kind. This is the paradox. What I call the free essence is actually the will. (The will is the power that initiates some idea, feeling or action.) Only the will is free. Initially the will freely chooses something, sets some sort of motion pattern in action, and this motion pattern once established will persist until stopped by some stronger motion pattern. This persistence is called inertia. Most people act always from inertia. Their actions are the result of some previous act of will freely chosen in the distant past and now automatically, inertically, persisting, the origin of which they no longer have knowledge. Thus they are bound by such actions. They are not free. When they say, 'I am free, I can do what I want' they have forgotten that 'want' was determined long ago and it may not be relevant in modern day conditions.

Eugene said, 'The purpose of the material world is to provide a resistance to the will'. And further, 'The resistance of the material world increases in proportion to the spiritual endeavour'.

One sees now why, to repeat, 'Freedom is having the ability to choose your own bondage'. For bondage you must have in order to be, and if you wish to be free, truly free, you must be able to choose the bondage, otherwise it will be chosen for you by another in order to gain power over you, which is not free.

The truly free being is free as the infinite intelligent spirit, God, is free. He is inside the circle and outside at the same time. To do this he vibrates from one to the other so rapidly it appears to be the one motion. This action Eugene calls 'Reflexive Self-Consciousness'. Very few people achieve it. All the world's adepts, the true spiritual leaders, the prophets of old, the founders of religions, the saints, the mystics, the great artists and scientists had it. God's goal is for everyone to achieve it. Who knows how long this will take? Ages? Aeons? No matter, for God is in no hurry for he has all eternity. And if he sees mankind will never get there, he will simply produce a form of life that will. But remember St. Augustine's early cry, before he achieved it, 'Lord make me perfect, but not yet!' The longer the individual waits before he starts on the road, the road ultimately leading to perfection and immortality, the more unintended suffering he will bear. For anything

46

short of this state of self-realisation, which is pure and constant joy, is suffering. (The purgative suffering he will suffer when on the path he bears gladly, for it is not resisted and so becomes a joy.)

Self-realisation, enlightenment, is a state of transcendent self-consciousness that in essence consists of being always in a balance between unconstrained freedom and constrained freedom, outside the circle and inside the circle simultaneously. As Jesus said 'When you make the two one and when you make the inner as the outer . . . . then shall you enter the Kingdom'. (Gospel of Thomas, 22), The inside is the free spirit, which is the true self of the being, the outside is his body, the material world. Yet from the universal aspect, the point of view of God himself, God as he is to himself, is free and outside, and God as the creation, as the material world, is inside. The creation is God's body to his free spirit, as man's body is to his free spirit. God's infinite free spirit is man's finite free spirit writ large: God's creation is man's body writ large.

So what is this Kingdom? Is it a place? Of course not, it is a state of being. The Kingdom of Heaven, according to Eugene, is 'equilibriated power', that is, the balance of the two forces, the outer and the inner, the free and the unfree (domed), the cause and the effect, the inner true self and the outer false self, the Big Self and the small self, the spirit and the material. When these two interpenetrate each other they create freedom.

Most people only concentrate on the material aspect of freedom, based on outward values. They usually ignore, for they know nothing about it, the inner, which is the original causer of freedom. The man in prison, bound in chains, if he has achieved self-realisation, can be more free than his jailor. For freedom is an inner state, not an outer one. If you are free in this inner mode nothing in the outer material world can affect you.

When you make the two one so that they interpenetrate each other, each becomes the other while still remaining itself. Thus from the universal spirit's viewpoint (God), he remains outside and free while intentionally binding himself by creating the universe. The universe is God limiting himself for the purpose of manifesting himself. Conversely, the man is free inside in his deep unconscious true self, his innermost spirit, while being bound, limited, in his outer physical body. God goes from the outside in, man goes from the inside out.

But why manifest at all? What is manifestation?

Manifestation is being. To be you must manifest. Without being there is nothing, that is, no things, no phenomena. Without being there is no actual awareness of oneself. Before being, before the creation, there is only an unformulated awareness of potentiality. That is why God creates. God wills to know himself in his fullness.

So Man, being derived from God and thus in essence a little god himself, also wills, when at his optimum level, to know himself in his fullness. He longs to return to his source, to his origin, to his Father. As Jesus said, 'I and my Father are one'.

Why this will to know oneself in one's fullness?

Because it brings harmony, it unites the inner with the outer and this is the only way to bring joy and peace. God is in this state eternally, he has achieved his goal, Man has a long long way to go, witness all the wars and conflicts everywhere. When the whole world is perfect, in total harmony in all its parts and modes, then we can say, 'His worship is perfect freedom', then we can say, we are truly free.

How does the world, how does the individual, achieve this perfect harmony? What is required?

The world, the universe, is already in harmony, for it obeys fully the laws of being — nature — which control and maintain its action. It is all of a piece, it is not individuated as man is.

Individuated.

That is the problem as far as man is concerned. For man is

individuated and controls himself as a separate being from all the other beings. This is what makes him different from the animal world. Man can think and reflect upon himself as a separate entity apart from all others. He then feels he must guard himself against these others. He can think ahead in a way animals do not, and foresees all kinds of possible dangers. Thus he, so to speak, binds his cloak more tightly around himself as a protection and thus does not relate fully and openly with his fellows and does not relate fully with the phenomena he calls the universe. In fact, deep down, he feels everyone and everything is a potential enemy. So he regards all other beings with suspicion and all nature as fit to conquer by all means possible and as fit to use for his own pleasure and advancement. He does not see that all the world is from one source and that this includes him. There is something, a power, which is greater than himself and this power, most importantly, is supremely intelligent. He does not like this thought and so ignores it and goes on living in his small and privated way. Thus he never achieves freedom, for he refuses to recognise the Truth.

A man, who died in 1987, has been mentioned several times in this brief writing. In conclusion therefore let me state that my simple and humble effort, written mainly for my own enlightenment, is light-years away from the wisdom of this man who is, for me at least, a shining beacon for the coming enlightenment of mankind. If you would wish to be free, study him. His words are gold.

This man is Eugene Halliday.

Book 6

LAST LETTER FROM A FATHER TO HIS SON

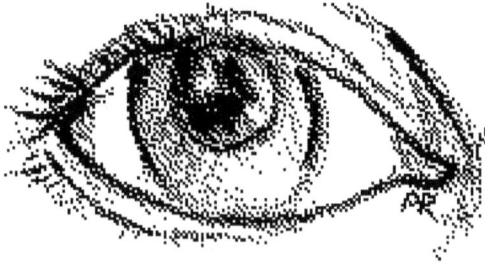

Dear Son,

It's over ten years since we met. The last I heard of you, you were in South America working on a project to halt the deforestation of the Amazon rainforests. A worthy task but largely vain, I fear.

I am now at a very advanced age, although fortunately still in excellent health. But at this age one must expect the Grim Reaper at any time. So one lives from one day to the next. It is actually a most marvellous time; one can say the best time of one's life. One has no longer to struggle with life; one has worked out to one's own satisfaction the answers to that life that have troubled one and, in short, one has made one's peace with the world and awaits the end, whenever it may come, with equanimity. I think of those marvellous words of Hamlet's:

> If it be now, 'tis not to come;
> If it be not to come, it will be now;

If it be not now, yet it will come.
The readiness is all.
Since no man knows aught of what he leaves,
What is't to leave betimes?

And so I thought I would try to answer, and also partly for myself as a last testament of my beliefs, reached after a lifetime's study, that very simple question you once asked as a boy of ten, looking up at the star clad night sky; 'Dad, what does it all mean? Why is there a world?' Do you remember? Then we were called in to dinner, you tripped on the step and broke your leg, you were rushed off in the ambulance, and the question never got answered. But I never forgot it, and now all these years later, in my twilight years, I will do my best to attempt an answer.

* * * * *

'Dad, what does it all mean? Why is there a world?' What a question! How does one begin to answer such a query? And why do I still remember it? Because it was the self same question I had asked myself at your age. When I heard you utter those words I saw myself again, no older than you, looking up in the darkness and seeing a myriad of twinkling lights and thinking, Why are they there? How did it all come about? Surely the most natural state of affairs is for there to be nothing, not something. Why should there be anything at all? Does anyone know the answer?

And as the years went by it became my lifelong study to find that someone; someone who KNEW. What a search it was! Have I found him? Yes – I have found scores, hundreds, thousands, who knew and who know. In fact I have found that the answer has always been known since remote antiquity, since prehistoric times. And it's not forgotten even now. The answer is still there, staring you in the face, if only you know where to look. Where to look? And how to look. Ah, yes, that's the problem.

I started by reading all the well-known living and dead thinkers, philosophers and scientists, and also all the theologians and the various orthodox religious texts. Some were very hard to follow; I found a million theories, conjectures, hypotheses. The scientists said it did not come within the scope of their investigations, and only concerned themselves with the How of things rather than the Why. The theologians said man could never know the ultimate reality and fell back on trusting in Faith and God. The orthodox religions had a certitude, but were so full of miracles, virgin births, risings from the dead, and so forth that I couldn't see how a modern mind, of whom I counted myself as one, could possibly accept such claims as true and valid.

I became an agnostic, and then an atheist. I believed in reason and reason alone. Whatever was put forward had to be accepted by logic alone.

At a certain point I came across a saying -- Hermetic, as I later discovered -- When the pupil is ready the master will appear.

And shortly after, he did.

My life immediately changed. I knew at once as soon as I walked into the room where he sat informally chatting to a group of young men and women. Here was a master indeed.

He was about forty with a short trimmed beard; his eyes were humorous and twinkling, and very piercing, with a gaze that went through you like a dagger. You could hide no secrets from this man. Yet his whole demeanour was gentle and benign. His forehead was high and domed and his hair dark. He described himself, as I later discovered, quite simply as an artist.

He sat on a chair in the small kitchen in front of the unpretentious ceramic tiled fireplace on which he drew simple geometric diagrams as he talked. The sketching and talking were of a piece, cohering as one. And what talk! He spoke with complete fluency and authority. No matter what the subject — and the discussion roamed ocean--wide over every topic imaginable — his discourse was a seamless garment that had no hems or joins. His speech was a continuum with no discrete parts, totally holistic. I had never heard talk like it. Listening to him I began to realise what it must have been like to have known Socrates, Jesus, the Buddha.

Over time I learnt he knew of and had studied every great thinker of the past, but more to the point, he made me see things from a completely new angle. I slowly began to experience a total metanoia, a 180 degrees shift of vision. I saw the esoteric meaning of every exoteric statement of the theologicians, mystics, and philosophers. I saw that the ancient myths and legends contained universal and cosmic truths of the utmost profundity.

I began to take up again my studies from this new viewpoint and it was as if a vast landscape had opened before me that had before been veiled in dense clouds of fog. The man, whom I shall call simply 'The Master', said, 'Study the Great themselves. Read their actual works, don`t waste time on what others think they wrote, but what they actually wrote. They wrote truths; most commentators distort those truths, either through ignorance or through an ambition to promote their own cleverness and knowledge'.

So I did this, and saw that they knew, just as the Master knew. This truth was everywhere if you looked in a certain way. All that was needed was a shift of vision, a change of angle. Was that what Jesus meant by – 'Except ye be born again ye shall not see the kingdom'? And again, 'The kingdom of heaven is within you'? Was that also what he meant by 'Repent'? I was told by the 'Teacher' to study the origin of the meanings of words, and I found repent meant simply rethink. So to repent is just to rethink one's point of view.

One has to climb to the top of the mountain to get the whole view. And then what a vista opens before one's eyes. One begins to see as the Master sees, as all the ancient Sages saw, as all the present Sages still see. As everyone has it in them to see. It is as if there are two worlds. The world the ordinary man sees, and the world the sage sees. It is only the one world but seen from two different perspectives, two different modes of seeing. The sage sees the world whole, the ordinary man partially. William Blake says, 'The fool sees not the same tree the wise man sees'.

Once seen from the sage's point of view, everything drops into place, everything coheres, everything becomes a seamless continuum, and all doubt falls away. 'The truth can make you free', says Jesus.

Then what is this truth, this viewpoint? How does one get there? The Hermetic doctrine says, 'As above, so below', and 'Man is a microcosm of the macrocosm'.

Why did whoever it was make the world? What is it all for? When and how will it end? To answer this we must go back to before the beginning, when there was nothing there.

What follows is my answer to this question. I hope it goes some way to clearing up that posing question you asked all those years ago, and have now either forgotten or it still nags at you. I have called it simply 'Credo'. I cannot prove it. It is simply my belief after a lifetime of thinking on these things. Take it or leave it: believe it or not as you wish. All I ask is you read with an open mind and consider if it seems logical to you, remembering it is what all the great minds of the past — and more and more of the present — have taught and believed. It is the considered wisdom of the ages and therefore not to be lightly dismissed. Also remember Occam's Razor, the principle of the medieval philosopher, who said, 'In any problem with a number of solutions, the simplest is the most likely to be correct'.

At the end I give the names of three contemporary writers I recommend.

CREDO

There is a 'somewhat' behind all phenomena and that is all that there is. All phenomena, visible and invisible, are functions of, and part of, this 'somewhat'. There is nothing other. This 'somewhat' can be thought of as energy; as power; as a life force; as a 'primum mobile'; as a first cause; as ultimate reality. Yet it is not a 'thing'. It is formless; it is nothing (no-thing).

However, this 'somewhat' is sentient. It is not a blind and purposeless 'somewhat'. It feels its own essential essence. It has no name, for it is prior to and anterior to the naming process, though men have given it many names — the Absolute; God; the Godhead; Brahman; Tao; Allah; etc.

If this 'somewhat' is sentient and has a purpose, what is this purpose?

Because there is nothing except itself, it has no enemies. It is alone (all one), and can do anything it wills. But one thing it cannot do; it cannot cease to be. It can never, so to speak, commit suicide.

And it is alone — 'alone, alone, all all alone on a wide wide sea'. And this aloneness is a terrible thing. This 'somewhat' feels its aloneness and an ache arises in it as of a woman aching to be filled, a womb aching to be filled. This 'somewhat' is a sentient void, an abyss. It has a choice. It can act or not act.

If it decides not to act, it remains as it is, a void, an abyss, yet content within itself. Nothing can destroy it. It can never die. And nothing happens. It is a mere potential. Eternally, Forever.

If it acts, it can do something, be something. It can make something, it can create. It can make actual what is in 'potentia'.

It can discover what is in itself. Although it already knows this, but in a sentient, that is, a feelingful way, not a fully formulated way. It feels a will to actualise its own potential, to manifest it, to 'bring it out into the open' as it were.

Yet now a problem arises. Out of what can it create? A potter needs his clay, a sculptor his marble, a painter his canvas. Yet there is only this 'somewhat'. Where is his clay, his marble, his canvas? He has only himself; there is no other. He must become his own clay; he must be both potter and clay. He wills to make something and there is only himself out of which he can make it.

The ancients symbolised this nameless 'somewhat', who was prior to creation, as a serpent running free. This serpent makes a wavelike motion as thus: ~~~~. This is a translating motion. It never crosses itself, or visits the same place twice. It is a breathing or pulsing. Also, whatever is experienced in one area is simultaneously experienced everywhere. Every motion or change of motion is everywhere felt and experienced simultaneously. This is what is meant by 'eternity'. There is only a continuous 'now'. It is a state prior to and anterior to 'time'; although the very words 'prior' and 'anterior' are themselves 'time' words. This state can never be described in words, for words are definitions, are part of the serialization process which only comes into existence with time, which itself only comes into existence with creation, and creation has not yet started. We can know of this state by feeling it in our own substance, rather like this 'somewhat' does, for we ourselves are derived from and are part of this 'somewhat'.

When the 'somewhat' decides to create, it turns its translating motion into a rotating motion. It crosses itself. It goes from to . (This is the move from Aries the Ram to Taurus the Bull — or Ball, the first two signs of the Zodiac symbology.) As it does this it creates a duality within itself. The energy, or power, or force, contained within the circumscribed zone is cut off and deprived; it is bound in by the walls of the circumscription. There is now an 'inner' and an 'outer'. The outer is free and is moving into the rotating, or bonding (bounding) zone, and the inner is bound and inside its cell — or self — and struggling to get out. These two states, the free and the bound (free-dome) exist simultaneously. The ancients called the free state Jupiter and the bound state Saturn — Satan.

This process, by which the translating motion moves by its own will into the rotating motion is the first FALL described in mythology and the main religious systems in the world.

This 'somewhat' has crucified itself; it has made itself into a stone, which signifies 'self-crucified-one' (self-T-one). It has made itself into a stone in order to create a substance out of itself on which to actualise its own potential.

It has become a duality, yet still remains one. The Hindu word for this is advaita (not-two). It has become two wills; the will to become something and the will to escape from the something back again into the nothing. Both at the same time. To think of one of these wills in isolation from the other is to be guilty of an abstraction; both occur simultaneously. And this

56

twofold motion, back and forth, in and out, is the secret of existence. This is why conflict and contraries are necessary to life. 'Without contraries is no progression' says William Blake. 'Opposition is true friendship.' 'Be my enemy for friendship's sake.'

The no-thing, which is free, longs to become something, and yet as soon as it has become something it feels its bound and separated state and longs to return again to its original free state.

This process is the origin of the universe (one-turning). The universe, creation, is the bound aspect of the 'somewhat'. It is that aspect of reality contained within the circumscription. And that which men call God, Allah, the Absolute, etc., is that aspect of reality which is outside the circumscription. God, Allah, the Absolute, is Jupiter. The universe, creation, is Saturn (Satan). Creation is to be 'cratered', that is, encircled, encapsulated in a crater. Creation is Hell, that is, to be held in. The whole world is crucified, hanging on a cross. A cross symbolises the intersection of opposing forces, the free and the bound. It has been truly said that 'Freedom consists in having the ability to choose your own bondage'. Existence implies bondage. God, in order to exist, which is a necessary corollary of his being able to manifest, freely accepts his bondage.

This is the significance of Christ, who deliberately and literally hung himself on a cross to bring to the attention of humanity this truth. 'Take up your cross daily and follow me.'

We are all crucified merely by existing. We cannot exist at all unless we are crucified. We are free spirits in circumscribed bodies. That is our glory and our bondage.

And the one who is most free and the most bound is the 'somewhat'. The universe is the 'somewhat' — God — crucifying himself for his own manifesting purposes.

As soon as he wills he can come down from the cross and the universe will cease.

57

According to the ancients there is a continual alternation between creation and non creation. In Hindu terminology the period of creation is termed a Manvantara, and the period of non-creation, or rest, is termed a Pralaya. It is also called the Day of Brahma and the Night of Brahma. Each alternation lasts millions of years — although in Pralaya time does not exist – a second is as a million years, a million years as a second. Eternity rules. Brahma is said to wake, then sleeps, the wakes again, and so on ad infinitum.

The human being is derived from and is part of this process, as are indeed all living beings. However the human being, who is a world in little, a microcosm of the macrocosm, occupies a unique position in the hierarchy of creation, a middle position, midway between the angels and the devils. (Man is able to reflect on his own origin, the animals don't.) The angels symbolise the free state and the devils the bound. The angels are those beings who are, so to speak, wholly on the 'good' side of creation, while the devils are wholly on the 'evil' side. Man is in the middle and has the ability to comprehend both the good and the evil. In other words, he is in the position to understand the nature of and purpose of the 'somewhat'. He is the 'Mediator of the Lord'. This is the meaning of the Messiah, the Mediator, the Messenger. He is Hermes, Mercury, Krishna, Christ. And we are all Christ, or can become so. Jesus himself was a being who understood this truth, a product of a long line of sages and prophets and deep seekers after truth. He made himself into a vehicle to express this truth. 'I and my Father are one.' God wills and purposes that every aspect of himself that he has created — out of himself — should eventually fully express himself. God wills to fully realise himself and express his full potential to himself and we, being part of him, are partakers of this process. 'We are Gods' when we put in the necessary work to become so. (Life is dynamic, not static.)

We can freely will in which direction to set ourselves. If we will to act in accordance to God's will, the Lord's will, then the Lord will back us up and assist us. He is, so to speak, waiting for us so to will, and he comes into us as a voice instructing us what to do. It is our own inner voice instructing us, yet the inner voice is really the Lord, for we and the Lord are one and indivisible -- though we must be sure it is not our own private selfish voice we hear, for the human's capacity for self deceit is infinite. If we so will we are immortal, for we are part of the Lord, and nothing can destroy the Lord, for there is nothing other than the Lord. And so the being loses his fear for he knows he is in the hands of a power greater than himself that will not let him down. 'Perfect love casteth out fear.' The point is we are all in this position but do not know it. Salvation consists in realizing we are gods and are immortal. However, to be as God, we must act as god, we must love all creation, for it is us and we are it. 'Love your neighbour as yourself.' It is not easy. In fact it is the hardest task in the world. Being in our own circumscribed cell — self — of our bodies, we identify with this body. This is the second Fall, the fall of Adam. We consider it over and against the other bodies we see all around us, and thus imagine the universe to be a mass of separate bodies, all fighting for survival against each other. In reality we are all facets of the one jewel, each raying out its own gleam of the one light. In reality we are all drops in the one ocean.

There is a paradox at the heart of creation and it is precisely this; the drop of water exists as itself and separate from all the other drops. In fact it is only by virtue of the fact that it is separate that it can exist as a drop at all. At the same time it is part of the ocean and owes its very existence to there being an ocean. No ocean, no drop.

When it knows this and remembers continually that it owes its final existence to the ocean, then it is immortal, for the ocean is immortal. When it tries to exist as a drop by itself then it simply evaporates in the fullness of time. (This does not mean it ceases to exist, for the evaporated drop will eventually fall to earth again as another drop, having mingled in its evaporated state with the rest of the air and drops and become a different drop from what it was originally.)

This whole concept of the meaning and purpose of life and our part in it has always been known. The ancients have described it in many and varied ways depending on their time and culture and language. It cannot be described in a straightforward 'scientific' way such that you listen or read it and say, 'Yes, I see that and understand', and then proceed on your way regardless. To truly understand it is to act upon it. It can never be 'proved' in the scientific sense of the word, for we are dealing here with a different order of apprehension of reality.

Science deals with the material world and how it works — we include in the material world the world of the mind, too, or at least the 'lower' mind, for that is also material. Science can only deal with this world. It cannot have anything to say about the non-material world, the invisible world, the spiritual world. (Ultimately science will 'prove' that the material world is born out of the non-material world. The something is born out of the nothing.) But the nothing is simply that which is 'not-a-thing'. Nevertheless, it 'is' in a mysterious way that is beyond our intellectual understanding, for the intellect itself is a product of the creative and evolutionary process.

Scientists are at present desperately trying to discover what consciousness is. They believe it to be a product of the physical brain process. Consciousness arises when the brain has become sufficiently complex; so say scientists. Actually it is the other way round; the brain is itself a product of consciousness. It can be better understood if we substitute the word 'sentience' for 'consciousness'. Sentience describes a feeling state and awareness of oneself. All living creatures are sentient, some more than others. When the evolving and unfolding sentience reaches a certain degree of self-awareness, a certain degree of complexity, then it can be called 'consciousness'. Consciousness is a formulated degree of awareness, a certain sharpness, a more narrowly focussed degree of awareness than is the more generalised field of sentience. The pre-creational sentience is seeking to express itself, and it builds ever increasingly complex systems in order fully to manifest its own inner glory. When the human physical brain is sufficiently developed it becomes able to express some of this; the brain will continue to develop and express ever greater and greater glories.

However deeply scientists delve into the mysteries of the brain they will never succeed in trapping consciousness. Consciousness, as presently understood by scientists, can only be considered a product of a physical brain. But it is not a product of that brain. It existed prior to that brain, but in a less formulated and articulated mode. It makes the brain in order to provide for itself a vehicle to fully become its own potential in actuality. Consciousness is complex sentience. Consciousness is the only 'non-mechanical' force in the universe, and as such scientists can never comprehend it as it transcends their own parameters of their area of investigation. (Although the latest 'quantum theory' and 'uncertainty principle' are getting remarkably close.)

There is a strange fact about consciousness. It is its own self-evidence. How can someone who is conscious prove it to someone who is not conscious? You are either conscious or you are not. If you know that you exist and are aware that you exist, what proof do you need that it is so? You know, and you know that you know. Only consciousness is aware of consciousness. Also, consciousness is not divisible. It is a continuum, an infinite field of sentience within which objects are observed. We are all 'within' consciousness and we are all partakers of the one consciousness. We are, so to speak, aspects of, rays of, the one consciousness. This consciousness is the 'somewhat'. All is consciousness or sentience. There is only sentience. Sentience is awareness, whether dim and dull, or sharp and focussed. We in our little bodies are as cells — selves — in the great body of the Lord.

Consciousness is unique. There is nothing like it except itself. It stands alone in reality; all else is derivative. The is why science can never 'get hold of it' as it can with all other phenomena. When science finally understands and comprehends what consciousness really is, it will know the secret of existence and the meaning of life. And when it knows this it will know that ultimately it knows nothing — no-thing. It will know that consciousness, sentience, the continuum, life, ultimately simply 'is' and is indestructible, and all one can do is lower one's head in humility and awe at the sheer inexpressible glory and wonder of it all and be thankful that one is, on however small a scale, a part of it.

This is Salvation. God is Love and Love is God: for love is to work for the optimum development of all being. That is what God does, and that is what we must do.

The three contemporary names I mentioned are as follows :--

1.   Owen Barfield 1898 – 1997.
2.   Rudolf Steiner 1861 – 1925.
3.   Eugene Halliday 1911 – 1987.

This is the Master I mentioned: — a truly great and brilliant man whom it was a aprivilege to know. Others have said he is one of the great spirits of our time.

All can be found on the Internet. Look them up. Read their works.

Well, son, that's it. That`s all I have to say. Accept it or not as you wish. All I can state is I have lived by these beliefs and they have stood me in good stead throughout a long life.

I commented at the beginning that your work on the Amazon rainforests was a worthy task but largely vain. I was wrong. Carry on; it matters not whether you succeed or no. The motive is all. The Lord knows his own.

Your Ever Loving Father.

I and my Father are one.
My Father works and I work.
Into His hands I commend my spirit.

Christ.

Book 7

MYTHOS AND LOGOS

Truth is one, the sages speak of it by many names

The Vedas

Mythos and Logos are two Greek words which originally had almost identical meanings but in the course of time have slowly drifted apart and now have completely opposite meanings. The original meaning was 'a tale', 'something told', 'speech', 'to tell' etc. At some early date — I think the first reference is in Homer, a mythical figure reputed to have lived some 800 years before Plato and Socrates — 'mythical' began to take on its current usage of 'poetic', 'fanciful', 'legendary' and logos to 'prosaic', 'order', 'true'. This has now become so deeply embedded that 'myth' now means something imaginary and untrue while 'logos' means something real, logical and therefore true. These two opposing meanings of the same essential and ultimate reality have now become the mindset of the current age and are — to me at least —

responsible for most of the ills afflicting the modern world. That world discounts utterly and ignores completely the 'mythical' element of reality, totally misunderstanding its true significance and instead puts its trust and belief in what it considers to be the only reality, i.e., that which can be explained by reason and logic. 'In the beginning was the Word' is the opening sentence of John's gospel. The original Greek has 'logos' for 'word'. In the beginning was the Logos. Logos is logic, word-reason, ratio, rationality, order. And order comes through the word. But behind and prior to the necessary order comes something else which one can call the poetic and intuitive. One can express these two words, which ultimately are the same truth yet in two different modes, as Mythos = Yin, and Logos = Yang. Mythos = negative, darkness, the night, and Logos = positive, light, day. Mythos = the moon, female, and Logos = the sun, male. Mythos = intuition, heart-feeling, and Logos = reason, head-feeling. (One ignores one's heart-feeling at one's peril.)

Mythos and Logos are the two modes of the ultimate reality. Behind these is the ultimate reality itself which is, in itself, in its own essence, beyond the comprehension of the human mind. The trouble with today is that logos, reason, is regarded as the only true way forward in trying to grasp the nature of reality. It ignores the part mythos plays which is equally, if not more so, important. The world can only be understood as a duality which is yet one. Everything implies its opposite. Historically speaking mythos comes before logos, though the latter is implicit in the former. In Christian terms, Mythos is the Father and Logos is the Son. Mythos is holistic, the original whole, Logos is subsequent and separative.

In very early times truths were understood in terms of myths, while now they are understood in terms of science. Both systems are equally valid from their respective viewpoints. The idea that myths are just primitive fairy tales told to children or to illiterate savages around a camp fire cannot be further from the truth, and is the result of Darwin and Victorian theories of ever increasing progress from barbarism to civilisation. In fact, myths contain extremely precise cosmological and astronomical information that is the equal of modern knowledge and in many cases surpasses it. The ancients knew such things as the diameter and circumference of the earth, the distance of the earth from the sun and from the moon, and a multitude of similar facts of which they are presumed by modern scholars to know nothing, sitting in their caves and grunting like apes.

Humanity is hierarchical. The world today is a mixture of primitive societies and highly civilised ones. So also in the ancient world. Modern scholars spend their time and energy digging up old bones and fossils and basing their conclusions accordingly. They ignore the amazing structures still standing, Stonehenge, the Pyramid of Giza, Angkor Wat, Machu Picchu etc., simply because they cannot explain them. But all of them and many more contain, when decoded, truths far in excess of modern knowledge, truths about the origin and meaning and purpose of life which have always been known and which are just in the very early stages of being rediscovered. Even in the relatively modern days of the Renaissance, namely the 16th and 17th centuries, these truths were known, witness Shakespeare, Jacob Boehme, John Dee and many others. William Blake in the 19th century knew, though he was regarded by his contemporaries as mad.

These truths were not discovered by the ancients by empirical and logical methods, as they would be today, but were revealed to ancient men and women in dream and vision in the same way the shamans of primitive tribes do today. These shamans and sorcerers still possess some of the clairvoyant characteristics of their ancient forbears.

The ancients did not think logically as we do today; they thought psychically and intuitively, and so naturally expressed themselves in myths. The myth is female; logic and science is male. The myth expresses a particular aspect of a cosmic truth in the form of a story, which entrances the normal listener or reader while conveying a deeper meaning for a more enlightened one. Myths are a more universal and all embracing way of enshrining these truths, for as long as the main elements of the story remain constant, everything else can be varied infinitely according to the culture and mores of the society concerned. Hence myths last and are continually passed on from one generation to another. They contain eternal truths which are constant, while scientific truths are relative, being constantly revaluated and updated.

Shakespeare's plays are examples of modern myth which enshrine basic truths about the human condition and bring them into correspondence to the greater universal condition. Microcosm and macrocosm both act in accordance with the identical laws of being. Hence their enduring popularity and ability to be transposed into whatever is the current fashion of the day. Shakespeare's plays were the popular entertainment of the time, which are yet of all time. Whoever wrote them was a true mouthpiece for the ever present and authentic author, the creator of the universe. And so with all myths.

Actually all stories, of which the modern medium is the cinema and television, cannot help telling tales which are variants of the ancient myths, witness 'Star Wars', 'Jaws', Tolkien's 'Ring' cycle and so on. These tales are immensely popular yet few realise they are in essence retellings of tales as ancient as humanity itself. The basic story is the ever-recurring tale of the quest of fallen man on his adventure back to wholeness and self-realisation and on the way overcoming the monster hidden deep in his unconscious and, if successful, finally winning the hand of the beautiful maiden who is his soul and true self. In order to conquer the series of ordeals placed before him he has to use his reason, his logos, which usually appears as some magical helper, an animal, an old crone, or often an obscure old man. These tales are universal and will always exist for they speak to a deeper reality than that of logic or reason.

'The heart has its reasons that reason knows not of' as Pascal says. Reason (logos) is of the head while mythos is of the heart. And mythos is before logos. The heart, which is holistic, all embracing, poetic, creative, is prior to logos which is separative, prosaic, non-creative. Mythos is thus generalised and undifferentiated, embracing all things, and though knowing all things, left to itself would dissolve into an emotional and phantasmic void. Reason, order, is needed to organise and separate it all out into its various categories and arrange it into its hierarchical structures. Both are needed and both are emanations from the invisible original power and intelligence which is the source of all.

What the present day western culture fails to take into account is that the reason (logos), while ordering and accounting for all phenomena can actually of itself create nothing. It is written, 'Behold I create all things new'. Reason can create nothing, all it does is compare one thing with another and so judges them as fit for purpose or not. To create one needs mythos. Ask any artist. Ask any woman. The true artist is androgyne, a man-woman, mythos working harmoniously with logos. This is the true and only way of the world.

Book 8

THE PROBLEM OF EVIL

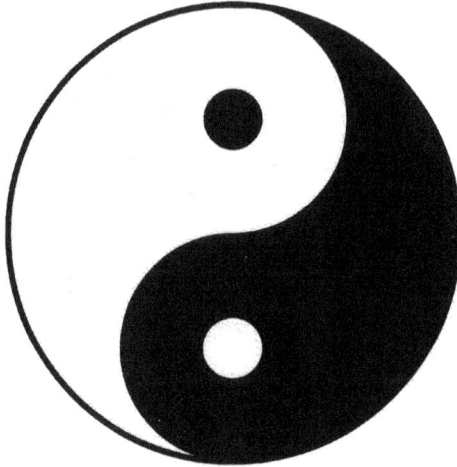

This is the supreme symbol which expresses the duality of the world, the light and the dark, the good and the evil, each of which needs the other in order for the physical world to exist. Each interpenetrates the other, as is shown by the dark spot in the light and the light spot in the dark. The symbol is the Wheel of Life, alternating up then down, always turning, which is creation, which is Life. The Yin Yang is the symbol of Finity, behind which, and not shown for it is invisible, is Infinity, the Primal Cause transcending light and dark, which is perfect peace and rest and, above all, Absolute Love.

————————————————————

I approach this problem with some trepidation, for it is a very difficult and charged one to come to grips with in the hope of any reasonably and easily understood conclusion. If God or some Supreme Intelligence exists and is all good, how can he permit evil to exist? This is how the question is often put and there appears to be no answer that fully satisfies. Many people thereafter cease to have any faith or belief. 'If such a God exists then I don`t want any part of him.'

I feel very poorly equipped to attempt any answer and lay myself open to the charge of presumption and arrogance, yet because I have myself wrestled with the question over many years I feel emboldened to do so, if only to satisfy myself, though with a great humility for I know I tread in the path of others immeasurably greater then I. Ultimately, I think, the full and true answer can never be given for it is embedded in a great mystery which can never be explained, only felt.

For me, the question can be approached from two angles, from the head and from the heart. The head will give the rational answer, which is based on the actual structure of the universe and is found in all ancient teachings and traditions. The heart is more difficult for it involves the aforesaid mystery and the immense suffering and the terrible tragedy of evil, which yet culminates in the final paradox of the joy of acceptance.

Let`s start with the rational, the answer of the head, the cold and impersonal reason for evil. Shortly, this answer is that evil is necessary for there to be any form of manifestation, for there to be any world at all. Evil, from this aspect, is simply 'separation'. Separation from what? From the 'Whole' of which it is a part and from which it originated. This Whole is the God or Supreme Being who is regarded as intelligent, is the only ultimate reality, and is the cause of the universe and who is the universe while yet remaining not the universe. Perhaps one way to try and grasp this difficult concept is to consider your own being. Think of your body as a tiny universe and your consciousness, your awareness of yourself, as a god coordinating and governing it. Or think of yourself as a king living in your kingdom. As a king you are not your subjects yet you are intimately a part of them and your very existence as a king depends on them. They are a part of you, and you are a part of them, while remaining infinitely above them. So it is with God.

God is the king and the world is his realm. God, while still himself, is also his realm. You, while still yourself, are also your body. Yet you are more than your body. When it dies you do not die. As God is immortal, you are immortal.

(The church does not accept this. For it, God and the world are separate and different entities. The church considers the world as evil, for it is separate from God and thus deprived of partaking in his glory. And for the materialist all of this is meaningless, for to him everything comes about by chance, accident and what he calls 'random selection'. But I write from the standpoint of a believer in a Supreme Intelligent Power which is the ultimate only reality. If there is no such power then there is nothing, so I believe. So a materialist or a believer in orthodox church doctrine need read no further.)

Now, no Supreme Power, no God, then no universe. But if that is the case it follows that if there is a God and if there is a universe and if there is evil then God is responsible for the evil. If there is nothing without God then God makes the evil just as he makes everything else. The realisation of this fact is what puts so many people from acceptance of God`s reality.

However, it requires a little more explanation. God is spirit, a formless nothingness which is yet aware of itself. It is not a thing, it has no form — just as your consciousness has no form — which is why we call it nothing, i.e. no-thing. God does not exist, as we use the term exist, for to exist implies having a form. Yet God 'is' in some mysterious way beyond our rational understanding. We can get the merest glimpse of what this state is and how it feels to be in it if we consider our own consciousness, for our consciousness is a replica in miniature of the world consciousness which we call God. The ancient Hermetic maxim has it, 'As above so below: as below so above'. Our consciousness is a tiny living spark of the all-embracing living fire which is reality, which is God. So we are actually identical with God, for we are a part of him and are him although, of course, from our tiny perspective we comprehend only a miniscule part of what God comprehends. One spark can be said to be nothing compared to the whole fire, yet it is of the identical essence of the fire and so can be said to be the fire in miniature. And ancient tradition asserts that as one climbs slowly through suffering and various trials and becomes of increasing worthiness and increasing love of all living things and overcomes one`s sense of isolating self absorption more and more, then

70

one's consciousness widens and opens out and becomes more and more comprehensive as one becomes more and more Godlike. Yet, paradoxically, the more Godlike one becomes the more humble one becomes. Dante's great poem, The Divine Comedy, and especially the final canto Paradiso, is a marvellous description of this process.

Let us return to the initial creation. God is an intelligent, formless, awareness of himself. There is nothing but this awareness. There is nothing else, the universe has not yet come into existence. God is all alone. All is darkness, all is chaos. Yet deep in this darkness is a living light, deep in this chaos is a burning desire to be. 'To be' is a doing, God longs to be, to be a form, God longs to see himself. Now you can never see yourself except by looking in a mirror. The universe is God's mirror. To see yourself, to exist, you need to become a form, a shape, you have to manifest. The universe is God's Manifestation.

And this is where the evil comes in. For manifestation is separation. God, in order to manifest, to see himself, has to alter from being formless and invisible to becoming formed and visible. So now we have two states, the invisible and the visible. The invisible can see the visible, while the visible cannot see the invisible. Your eye can see, yet it cannot see its own eye. The 'I' can never see itself, only its reflection. God, who is the supreme 'I', can only see himself through his reflection, which is the universe.

Thus the creation of the universe begins with a duality, a separation from the original unity. This duality is expressed in a myriad of different modes: negative and positive, the yin and the yang, female and male, passive and active, Plato's the Same and the Other, Mother and Father, and finally The Whole and the Separation from it. This duality, being in essence a unity, means that to consider one to the exclusion of the other is an error. Neither exists without the other, each needs the other in order to 'be'. Light implies Dark, High implies Low, Good implies Evil, attraction implies repulsion. You cannot have one without the other. And behind this duality is the original Essence, the Ultimate Intelligent Power which is God, who is both and yet neither. Hindu tradition has a word 'Advaita', usually translated as 'not two'. So from this aspect it is not one but it is also not two. It transcends both. One begins to see why something beyond mere rational understanding is required, something akin to — a much misunderstood word these days — mystical knowledge, is required to begin to understand something of the mystery. For mystery it certainly is.

Now there is a constant battle between these two forces, the positive and the negative, the good and the evil, attraction and repulsion. A contemporary of William Shakespeare, Jacob Boehme the 'humble German master cobbler', spoke of the two forces as the Love of God and the Wrath of God. And William Blake speaks of the two as Energy and Reason, the former as the power that initiates and drives all activity, and the latter as the restraining power of that activity. He says, 'Without contraries is no progression'. Evolution proceeds by each interpenetrating the other. The energy left to itself, as Shakespeare says, will 'as appetite, an universal wolf, so doubly seconded with will and power, must make perforce an universal prey, and last eat up himself". The reason is needed to restrain and to order that power into suitable activities. Yet the reason left to itself will so order the energy that eventually it will seize up and become totally immobile. Lastly William Blake says, 'Attraction and repulsion, energy and reason, love and hate, are necessary to human existence'. Love is of the Whole, Hate, or Evil, is of the Part, is separation from the whole.

What does it mean to say 'Evil is of the part, is separation from the whole?' How can separation be evil? Evil is to act entirely from one's self and for one self and with no consideration for others. As each part is a replica in miniature of the universal whole, so it may, and usually does, consider itself to be a whole entity, complete within itself, and so act accordingly as if it is the whole without regard to the rest. The mass of individuals think the world to be made up of other individuals, each a whole like themselves, and thus forced to struggle against these others for survival. This is an illusion, of course, for each individual in reality is a single cell in the body of the whole, which is the universe, in just the same way as each single cell is in the physical body of the individual. One can see the reason for this illusion for each cell — or self — is an exact copy in miniature of some aspect of the Whole, and is in essence the whole, and as the whole is free and alone, so the cell self-reflects this. It has been said, 'God is free so when he creates creatures they are necessarily free also'. God must allow his creatures to be free, to be free to make choices, otherwise they would be slaves. And God does not deal in slaves.

What are the choices that God allows his creatures to make? They are the same choices that God himself made when forming the universe, only in the reverse order. God made the choice to limit himself, to move in a series of emanations downwards, from the whole to myriads of parts, to separate individuated selves: the individual has to make the choice to move upwards, from his limited and separate self to the greater Self, which is the whole, which is God.

Only he may, and usually does not, do this. Instead he chooses — though chooses is perhaps not the right word, for to choose well requires a modicum of wisdom and understanding, not ignorance, which is the normal human state — to simply remain as he is, a separate, limited, isolated being amongst a mass of similar beings. Here lies the true source of evil. He is separate, he is, as the church has it 'in original sin'. But the word 'sin' is the English rendering of the Greek word 'hamartia' which simply means 'to miss the mark'. The mark, or the bullseye, is the return to the whole while remaining oneself. The man in the street does not do this, he does not know what he is 'missing' so he always misses the mark. To be oneself and yet at the same time to be greater than oneself, so that one is nothing and yet everything, is to truly live, is to be truly free. Anything less than this is to be a slave. But the ordinary man does not realise this and so remains a slave.

To what is he a slave? The physical material world in which he 'lives and moves and has his being' is but a shadow of the real world, of which he has no knowledge. Plato's myth of the Cave is the best symbol I know which vividly expresses this. If you are not aware of the myth, here it is:--

A group of men and women live in a cave. They pass the time watching the moving pictures — television? — passing and re-passing on the cave wall in front of them. There is light, which they ignore, behind them. One day one of them climbs up to examine the source of the light and finds it leads to a way out of the cave. He clambers out and finds he is in another world full of sunshine and with other beings moving about and casting their shadows on the wall of the cave. He excitedly re-enters the cave and tells his companions of his discovery of the real world outside. But they don't listen and continue to watch the shadows.

This is the normal way of the world. Human beings live in a shadow world. They never see the shining light, the truly splendorous and overpowering light of the real world which is above, beyond, and is yet in the ordinary world, and is also in their inmost heart. They never see the invisible in the visible. Jesus said (Gospel of Thomas, 22), 'When you make the two one, and when you make the inner as the outer and the outer as the inner and the above as below, then shall you enter the Kingdom'. Not doing this, thus they miss the mark. Thus they are in sin. Thus they are evil, not intentionally so but out of ignorance of the whole picture. Just as a child out of ignorance plunges his hand into the fire and so burns it, so does the ordinary man, the unregenerate man, sin by omission by not realising the course of his actions. 'Forgive them Lord, they know not what they do', uttered Jesus as they hammered nails into his hands. Could you forgive them as they were doing a thing like that?

Oh, love, love, the pain of the world is too much to bear! I die, I die.

So this, then, is evil. To miss the mark, to harm your fellow man, though with no idea of being evil, but out of sheer ignorance of the consequence of your actions. But what of the beings considered truly evil? What of Hitler, Stalin, Pol Pot, the terrorist, the serial killer. Are they not the true embodiment of all that we deem evil? Well, of course they are, but they are only extreme examples of the very ignorance of which I speak. Hitler did not think he was being evil when he attempted to exterminate the entire Jewish race. He just did so out of perverted ignorance, thinking he was carrying out an heroic deed by ridding the world 'of this accursed tribe who have caused all the evil in the world'. So, for other perverted reasons, with Stalin and Pol Pot, so with the terrorist, the serial killer. The Islamist terrorist thinks he is ridding the world of 'the accursed infidel', of American influence, and establishing Sharia law everywhere, which he thinks will produce peace on earth. The serial killer makes a choice between his pleasure at killing, which inflates his sense of power, over his knowledge of the universal law which says it is wrong to kill. He wants the pleasure that the power gives and thinks he can avoid the penalty. Yet deep down in their innermost selves all these types have an unease which they don't wish to confront, a hidden certainty of their wrongdoing. One cannot go against the Whole, the Self, without knowing in the depths of the soul what one is doing. When the self acts against the Self of which it is a part it sets up a disequilibrium and an imbalance which must be restored, and the self which has caused the fault knows that in the fullness of time it must suffer retribution in order to restore that balance.

When the self acts against the Self of which it is a part, it sets up a disequilibrium and an imbalance which must be restored. The self which has caused the fault knows that in the fullness of time it must suffer retribution in order to restore that balance.

The Greeks describe this process as hubris which is followed by nemesis. The Greek tragic plays, as also Shakespeare's, describe this process acting out marvellously. Pride goes before a fall, or as the saying goes, 'Every man gets his come-uppance', Mark Twain said in his inimitable way, 'No one gets out alive!' So evil always has to pay the price of trying to go against the whole.

Jesus said, 'Resist not evil'. A strange saying. What does it mean? As I understand it, it means that by resisting evil you create more evil, for evil being the act of separation, by resisting separation you create more separation. The way to resist evil is to absorb it into the Whole. This is the Way of Zen, of the Tao, of the eastern martial arts. 'Go with the flow.'

An American professor, Josiah Royce, 1855-1916, has some pertinent things to say. 'All finite life is a struggle with evil. Yet from the final point of view the whole is good. The Temporal Order contains at no one moment anything that can satisfy. Yet the Eternal Order is perfect. We have all sinned and come short of the glory of God. Yet in just our life, viewed in its entirety, the glory of God is completely manifest. These hard sayings are the deepest expression of the essence of true religion. — In the bare assertion of just these truths, that appear to our ordinary consciousness a stumbling

75

block and foolishness, the wisest of humanity in India, in Greece, and in the history of Christian thought, are agreed. — All things work together for good from the divine point of view: and whoever can make this divine point of view in any sense his own, just in so far sees that they do, despite the inevitable losses and sorrows of the temporal order.'

And Fabre d'Olivet, 1768-1825, says, 'The history of Mankind offers unceasingly the striking proof of this truth: that a particular evil is often necessary in order to bring forth a general good'.

A particular evil is often necessary in order to bring forth a general good. This is a hard saying. Is it true? And yet we all know of instances of what seems to be individual misfortune which yet turn out to be in the end for good. There is the story of the poor farmer whose only horse one day wandered away. His neighbours commiserated with him on his loss but the farmer simply shrugged his shoulders, 'Just the way of the world'. A few days later the horse returned bringing with him half a dozen wild horses. The neighbours congratulated the farmer on his luck. The farmer simply shrugged his shoulders, 'It's as it goes'. A week or so later the farmer's only son, in taming one of the horses, was thrown off and broke his leg. The neighbours bemoaned the farmer's misfortune. Who would now help him work the farm? 'It happens', said the farmer. Two weeks later, the son with his leg in plaster, a platoon of soldiers arrived conscripting all the young men to go to the war. The son was spared. The neighbours yet again congratulated the farmer. 'That's life', said the farmer.

So good can come out of evil. But often at what price! And often, too, the good comes so long after and is often so apparently unrelated to the apparent initial evil that it passes unnoticed. A tsunami roars over South East Asia and thousands die; a bomb is set off in a crowded market place and many die and are mutilated. How long will it be before the compensating and balancing good comes? And will it be noticed for what it is? Thousands are dying all the time. We all have to die. Dying is evil. Evil is everywhere. Hundreds of sensitive souls all over the world are committing suicide as they see no hope anywhere of stopping the terrible suffering.

And God, the Supreme Being is the cause of it all. For God is All. There is nothing except God. So the evil must be in God. Yes. But so must the good be, too. Also, God must suffer the evil as well as the good. God is in the perpetrator as well as in the victim. Truly it is all a great mystery which can never be fully understood by the poor human intellect. It can only be felt. It is often said, 'God moves in mysterious ways his wonders to perform'.

Ultimately the only answer is to reach a level of reality, the level of Absolute Love, where the duality is seen for what it really is, a level that transcends both good and evil, and, as I said at the very beginning, 'culminates in the final paradox of the joy of acceptance'. Yes, the joy of acceptance, for when it is experienced, hard though it may be for the ordinary soul to comprehend, it is joy, in fact it is greater than joy, it is a state of ineffable bliss that lifts the individual up into the very heights of God Himself where all is for the Good and always has been and always will be.

Let me end with the last two stanzas of Dante's immortal poem, the Divine Comedy. Here, at the very end of the last canto of the final part, the *Paradiso*, he reaches those utmost heights of ecstasy himself, beyond which a human cannot go. Here words almost fail him, great poet that he was:

> *Thither my own wings could not carry me,*
> *But that a flash my understanding clove,*
> *Whence its desire came to it suddenly.*
>
> *High phantasy lost power and here broke off:*
> *Yet, as a wheel moves smoothly, free from jars,*
> *My will and my desire were turned by love,*
>
> *The love that moves the sun and the other stars.*

Book 9 – A BOOK OF SONNETS

(1) A NOTE ON 'WHY WRITE SONNETS?'

I have several times been asked why, in these days of 'free-verse forms', I have chosen to express myself in the old-fashioned, worked-out, and rigid form of the sonnet. The Shakespearean sonnet, which is the variety I have here used, consists of fourteen lines of ten syllables each, broken into three quatrains rhyming alternately, and finished off and summed up by a rhyming couplet. Further, a sonnet should not meander or wander about; it should express a single idea or feeling, which is declared, elaborated, and then summed up in the final couplet.

It is precisely because it is so rigidly structured that I have chosen it. In attempting to get to grips with universal ideas it is necessary to be very particular. In trying to understand the imprecise, one must be precise, just as the sailor, in making his way across the chaotic and shifting form of the great ocean spaces, must be able to navigate. Navigation, although an art, is yet very precise.

You have to try to pin the idea down, even though you know it is essentially unpinnable, and the sonnet is a device to help you to do this. It makes you think clearly. You cannot write a sonnet whilst being washed over by vague feelings of an unformulated, mystical, 'Great Beyond'. You will drown in the abyss if you try. And yet, if your sonnet succeeds, it can actually give a glimpse of that 'Great Beyond'. For a fraction of a second the Infinite is caught in the net of the Finite. You have the merest glimpse of it before it darts out of the net and is away again. And yet you have seen it, and once seen never forgotten.

You have seen it because you had a net. And the net is the binding form of the sonnet. It could equally well have been the quartet, the fugue, the symphony, the terza rima of Dante, the rigid form of Greek Tragedy, the classical laws of composition of the great painters of the Renaissance. All art uses a net, for art is form, and form is a net. (The trouble with modern free-verse forms is precisely that, for the most part, they are formless and not compact or dense enough; they express very little in a large number of words.)

Another reason for using the sonnet is that its sound and rhythm is familiar to our ears and understanding, and we feel at home with it. Some of the ideas expressed here are maybe strange and difficult. It helps if they are cast in a familiar form. It certainly helps me as author! (For initially they were written for myself, in an attempt to clarify for my own understanding, various ideas that were floating vaguely about in my consciousness.) It gives some solid ground from which to advance into the unknown land.

In passing, to answer the possible objection that poems are about *feelings*, and not *ideas*, I would say that a poem is an idea expressed in such a way that it gives rise to feeling. An idea is an image that appears in the mind; a feeling is an experience of pleasure or pain that arises when that image is contemplated. The difference between a scientific statement and a poetic statement is that the first leaves you unmoved and the second does not. But they are both statements of an idea. Whether these sonnets are indeed poems, or merely versified statements of ideas, is for others to judge. There are some who say that a sonnet should only concern itself with that greatest of all feelings, 'Love'. Quite so. A sequence of no less than sixty 'Sonnets of Love' has been written, but they appear in another place.

Just as a sonnet explores the meaning of a single idea, so a sequence of sonnets takes that idea and expands the meaning to include various associated ideas. Because of this, each sequence should be thought of as a unified whole and read through in order.

The sequence on 'Consciousness' is dedicated to Eugene Halliday whose teaching, or my understanding of it, it embodies, and whose influence on my life is beyond expressing.

(2) TWELVE SONNETS ON
THE NATURE OF CONSCIOUSNESS

Dedicated to Eugene Halliday, whose teaching inspired them.

1   A circle draw and so confine a space;
Infinity beyond your line you'll see.
A larger circle draw, that to encase,
Beyond your second line it is still free.
Draw yet again and larger, yet again;
To capture try that which remains outside;
You cannot win, however much you strain,
Not even if your line be Cosmos wide.
For, though your line includes all that within,
It, at the same time, excludes that beyond,
And this exclusion you can never pin;
For ever it's external to your bond.
This shows a 'finite' there can never be
That doesn't presuppose 'infinity'.

2   They say there is no spirit, is no soul.
They say we're really only lumps of clay.
They say there is no sentient, prior, Whole,
But only purblind forces at their play.
The consciousness of men, and purposive,
Intelligent, awareness of an end;
Where in the universe do such things live?
They say, 'In aggregates of atoms, friend'.
'A single atom', then say I, 'can will,
Has consciousness, has purpose, is aware'.
'A single atom — no — and not until
The aggregate is complex', they aver.
If one atom is Zero — I am done! —
Then won't a million still a zero sum?

81

3   If it's not the seed it is not there;
You cannot graft it later on to suit.
Does any tree mature, of crop quite bare,
With boughs and branches minus any fruit,
And then, when fully ripe, and only then,
Decide upon what type of fruit shall fall,
Say, apple, orange, plum, and how and when,
Or, contrary, to bear no fruit at all?
Of course not! Everybody knows full well
Type and variety are there from start,
Patterned and predetermined in the cell,
Alive, yet still and potent in the heart.
So consciousness, fruit of the tree of man,
Was present in his seed when he began.

4   Then if it's in, orig'nally the seed,
(I mean the consciousness), what art or act
Inserted it, and whose lone, primal, deed
Initiated, dreamed, and made it fact?
Perhaps it didn't? Ah! Now here's a doubt!
Perhaps it was not consciousness that grew
Inside the seed, but t'other way about!
The Consciousness the seed internal knew.
Now here is — yes! — a thought to stagger reason!
Is consciousness then not what we suppose?
No potent bud appearing in due season,
Instead the field itself in which seed grows?
If so, before the seed, what can be higher?
The field in which it grows, for that is prior.

5   Is consciousness a thing, or is it that
Pure, sentient, field within which things are seen?
You at a thing may look and say, 'It's fat —
That's round,' — or 'Here's an object that is lean'.
You that looking do, are you a thing
As well? One object looking at another?
'Of course I am' you say, 'Here, touch my skin;
My body this is, and I'd have no other'.
But is your body you? Is it not true
That no thing at itself can look direct?
If you can look at it, it isn't you.
Yourself is conscious. With me you agree?
And consciousness does any of us see?

6   'The eye sees not itself but by reflection.'
Another, better, sonneteer has said;
And here's a thought inviting your inspection,
He may not only mean those in the head.
For there are eyes that gaze out on the earth,
And there's that 'I' you mean when you say 'Me'.
Then this consider — ever have from birth,
The 'I' that's you, or th'eyes with which you see,
Looked back upon themselves with direct gaze,
(Observer and Observed one of a kind).
Or rather, haven't they looked out on the maze
Of mirroring forms themselves to seek and find?
If no eye sees itself but through another
You do not know yourself but through your brother.

83

7   Each, all, and ev'rything that lives is conscious,
Though not all things self-consciously are so.
On earth, of beasts, is man alone audacious,
That Godly and Luciferan path to go.
The rock is conscious of itself as mass,
To change resistant, and inertia knowing;
The plant will push through earth and through morass,
From dark to light, and feel herself a-growing;
The beast is conscious of its hunger surge,
As soon its appetite knows how to stem;
But man inertia knows, growth, belly urge,
And well he knows he that he knows of them.
So Man, thus conscious of himself as man,
May on himself eflect; no other can.

8   A death's disintegration. When a form
Is split, reverts to its component parts,
Then it is dead, so broken by the storm
Of stimuli's bombarding, piercing, darts.
There is not any other death than this;
If no disintegration, then no death.
This so, then how give stimuli's darts a miss,
When one such dart is simply drawing breath?
But isn't it true that compounds only can
Disintegrate? May that be torn apart
Which has no parts to do so? How may Man
Escape disintegration then? The heart
Of it is this — a pure continuum find
Which has no parts, and you leave death behind.

9   Where then, may such continuum be found?
Where then, to search it out, do you begin?
To left? To right? Above? Or underground?
Around? Without? Inside or Out? Within?
Such searching will be fruitless, well you know,
For well you know it's not in any place.
The universe wide ranging you may go,
You'll not find a continuum in space.
It is, in fact, a thing you'll never see;
It never moves, yet's in perpetual motion;
It is confined within the smallest pea;
It reaches out beyond the farthest ocean.
Than it, there is not any other thing;
No thing itself, of all things it is king.

10   That's well,' you say, 'Yes, that is very well;
But what exactly do such fine words mean?
Explain "continuum" if you can. Please tell
How find a thing that never can be seen?'.
Well, here's the best that I just now can do,
But please read all the previous poems again.
Each one, in's different way, attempts a clue,
Like a miner tapping deep from vein to vein.
The truth is, this 'continuum's' that 'Out There',
Beyond the circle mentioned at the start;
And words define, and only can, the 'In Here';
The what's outside they cannot hope to chart.
Continuum, though by a diff'rent name,
With Sentient Field and Consciousness is same.

11   Between a wheel and its axle is a void,
That lets the spoke spin freely round the hub.
This space, this gap, must not be ever cloyed,
Or clogged, or closed, if wheel is not to rub.
It matters not how small this gap may be,
Essentially it's nothing, that's its strength;
And Nothingness is all Infinity;
It has no height or depth, no breadth or length.
This tiny space inside the wheel is one
And same as larger space outside the rim;
An Immanent and Transcendent union
Of little self with big Self, her with him.
This tiny space inside the wheel is you;
And that within and that without aren't two.

12   Identify with 'That within'; you're There!
You've traced the sacred river to its source!
You've found that pearl of wisdom, prize most rare!
Your journey's done; you've rounded, run, the course!
For 'That within' is you, the real you,
Not tied to body's temporary glove;
A nothing which is no thing, born anew;
A heliograph reflecting beams of love.
You have become a zonal reference centre,
Where consciousness, that infinite, sentient field,
That pure continuum, may know and enter
And feel itself through you. Your door unsealed,
There is not any other place to go;
There is not any other thing to know.

(3) THIRTEEN SONNETS ON THE GREAT INITIATES

1   The Great Initiates.

Since ages past, when men first walked this earth,
There have been those among them who have known
All that there is to know about the birth,
And growth, and dissolution of this stone
We call the universe; why, how, and when,
And for what purpose, and how long it will
Remain in being, and what happens then,
When all's at rest, and all is quiet and still.
These men we call the Great Initiates, and
Their message has been passed right down the line
From whispered mouth to mouth, and hand to hand,
Each generation's waters into wine
Thus being turned, then stored, a heady brew,
In jars of truth, reserved for worthy few.

2 Hermes Trismegistus.

The author of that great 'Book of the Dead'
Are you, thrice greatest Thoth, Egyptian sage;
Who taught men how to think and use their head,
And how the courses of the stars to gauge.
From lost Atlantis, now below the sea,
They say you came, and set your home up where
The centre of the earth is said to be,
In Egypt, and the Pyramids built there;
Those stone computers that are programmed so,
The road to man's true self they can reveal;
Those tombs to which a neophyte would go,
To test if he could tell the false from real.
When in the balance, Thoth, they're weighed together,
You write which tips the scales, the heart or feather.

3 Zarathustra.

The champion of the light against the dark,
Are you, great Persian seer; who life conceives
In dual terms, as conflict pure and stark,
Between that one who gives, and he who thieves.
Inside man's intellect's the battlefield;
There Ahriman the dark has pitched his tent
And, sceptic, whispers words of doubt, concealed;
Bewitching souls on private purpose bent.
But you have burned your selfish will away,
Pure Zarathustra, so ride forth to fight,
Upon your shield, as fierce as blazing day,
The true Ahura Mazda's searing light.
Within your book, the Zend Avesta's pages,
You fight, not for your time, but for all ages.

4   The Buddha.

Impassive, there you sit beneath your tree;
Upon your lotus leaf with gaze withdrawn.
Serenely sailing on your inner sea,
No more to die, no more to be reborn.
Son of a king, all comforts to your hand,
You left and took the beggar's path and bowl;
Forever searching for that golden land
Your tired heart knew was true home for the soul.
Within the palace, no, it was not there;
Without, in rags, barefoot — not to be found.
Th'extremes of wealth and poverty, this pair
Are steps alternate on the cyclic round.
The middle way then, that's the means to enter
The golden land; not right or left, but centre.

5   Lao Tzu.

A 'chink of light', if you'll forgive the pun
(Although to them yourself you were quite prone!)
Is how I always think of you. And fun!
With twinkle in your eye! A precious stone!
Five thousand words — yours is the shortest book.
Five thousand sparking facets of the real;
No sooner into focus — take a look!
Than out of sight again — it's turned on heel.
As water slipping through the hand's your 'way';
Not to be clutched, but felt as it flows past.
Your style not 'lucidly long-winded', say
Instead, 'concise ambiv'lence' is its cast.
The legend says you wrote your book and then
Rode through the gate and was not seen again.

89

6   Moses

Abandoned in an ark upon the water,
Decree of death upon your baby head,
Then found and nurtured by the Pharaoh's daughter,
You grew to be no slave, but prince instead.
With serpent-rod of power you outwitted
Egyptian magis, masters of the game;
You sent them plague on plague 'til was admitted
Supremacy of the Lord's most Holy name.
You led the people out into the wild,
First gave them freedom, then gave them the law;
Ordeal upon ordeal was on them piled,
To make a nation; squeeze out ev'ry flaw.
Then to the promised land they came at last,
But, Moses, you were not allowed to pass.

7   Pythagoras.

'The square on the hypotenuse' – your fame
On that familiar theorem rests, and yet
What other themes, much deeper, to your name
Are linked! How wide and how far-flung's your net!
You listened to the music of the spheres,
Their harmony exquisite filled your soul;
You taught, instructed, men to use their ears,
So that they heard, not one note, but the whole.
In 'number' is the principle and ground,
Your teaching went, upon which all things stand;
And 'number', which is 'intervals', is 'sound';
(Aren't mathematics, music, hand in hand?)
In Ancient Greece yours was a famous school,
Where 'God geometrises' was chief rule.

8   Socrates

What a lovely man you are, dear Socrates!
Against you no one has a word to say.
You gaily drank the hemlock to the lees,
And all the world's adored you from that day!
In your beloved city, Athens, where
You on street corners stood and taught the youth,
They had, to crucify, no Jesus there,
And so they picked on you for telling truth.
You wrote no books, your creed was in your life;
The Dialectic was your chosen tool,
(An art evolved from having as a wife
That shrew Xanthippe, calling you a fool!)
It's said Initiation you refused,
Preferring by your Daemon to be used.

9   Plato.

You at the feet of Socrates did sit,
And afterwards his teachings noted down;
And then you sought, and found, that form most fit,
The 'Dialogue', as dress for them and gown.
Yet you were no amanuensis mere,
But true philosopher in your own right,
Who showed those men who did from shadows peer,
The way to leave their 'Cave' and see the light.
You taught that objects of external sense,
As, instance, fruit we taste and smell and feel,
Are shadows, (spite of seeming solid, dense)
Of universal forms that are more real.
Although you'd exile poets from your state,
Weren't, Plato, you yourself as poet, great?

10   Shakespeare

Whoever thinks of England thinks of you,
For you are England's spokesman, England's face.
You bodied forth in words that point of view
That's so peculiar to the island race.
Who knows your creed? (what's ours you never ask)
Who knows, Perfidious Albion, where she'll go?!
Who's seen your face behind that Droeshout mask?
Is England smiling friend or smiling foe?
While others abide our question you are free,
It has been said – and is not England still
All things to all men? Boundless as the sea?
Like you, no written constitution, will?
As David, Psalm-like, you out-sang the birds,
And built the mind of England with your words.

11   Jacob Boehme

One day while walking in the fields a youth
A vision had; of nature clear as glass.
Transparent as an X-ray plate, the truth,
The bones, he saw within each blade of grass.
Two wills, he saw, contend for mastery,
And tension ever present 'tween the two;
And that to which the plant 'llowed victory,
Controlled the shape to which the plant then grew.
And each of us is such a plant that grows,
Identified with will of love or wrath;
Whatever sap that most within us flows,
We make our own, our signature, our cloth.
Thus, gentle Boehme, did you teach;
And minds of Newton, Goethe, Blake, did reach.

12   Jesus Christ

Great Spirit, of you I hesitate to write;
You tower a mountain range above them all.
The meekness of the lamb, the lion's might,
Meet both in you; and you reverse the Fall.
Others in ages past the way had shown;
But you, by willing to be crucified,
Not only showed, but did! Yes, you alone
Went to the end, gave up your life, and died.
The chemistry of the world you by that deed
For all time changed; its substance never more
Would be the same; in each man's heart a seed
Of love was planted he could not ignore.
Not only did yourself you resurrect,
Each man himself could now death's sting eject.

13   The Greatest of Them All

Within this teeming world in which we live,
Behind this lovely veil of time and space,
There's 'Him' slips through, however fine the sieve,
There's 'Him' who lives and breathes, though shows no face.
This 'Him' is no one, cannot be defined;
But he is sentient, of himself aware;
And for himself to see, from out his mind,
He bodies forth, as glass, this world so fair.
Then mirrored back, reflected, as a sun,
His motions —flashing forms — shine on the screen.
But these same forms, appearing one by one,
Are not this 'Him', for he is never seen.
As than this 'Him' there is not any other,
He's, while not them himself, both Father, Mother.

(4) FOURTEEN SONNETS ON
THE SIGNS OF THE ZODIAC

0   The Zodiac

The Zodiac's a sacred mystery,
Enshrining deepest truth within its heart.
The Zodiac's a cosmic history,
The key to evolution's hidden chart.
Wherever there is life, at work you'll see
Th'unfolding of a twelve-stage, cyclic plan;
Twelve signs along the roadway there will be —
That road that leads to Universal Man.
Each sign is symbol of a diff'rent stress,
Or emphasis, or accent, on the form;
Each sign is clothing in a diff'rent dress
To robe the latent smooth-skinned, waking corm.
But each of us, though one sign makes its mark,
We hidden have eleven in our dark.

1   Aries, the Ram

Beginning first, the pioneer, is Ram;
Called 'Cardinal Fire', he's heat in th'head, due north.
The sign where it is first declared, 'I AM!'
The place from which begins the going forth.
From out of chaos springs that first desire
To manifest, to wake, to be alive!
And this desire is rushing red hot fire;
To wake from deepest sleep you have to strive!
Full headstrong — bang! — the Ram is always right!
There are, as yet, no laws to say him wrong,
And knowing well this truth, he knows his might,
And 'I am right! Who cares for facts!' his song.
All forms of bondage spurning, Ram is free;
Out there in front, he's always first to see.

2   Taurus, the Bull

Behold! The Ram is in the thicket caught!
The energy that once was free is bound,
And in the Bull-ring's ready to be taught
To plant his feet four-square upon the ground.
With patience, industry, and quiet good-will,
Upon his tour, the Bull, acceptance learns;
The Bull's-eye seeking, centre small and still;
His strength the while secreting as he turns.
That strength, unleashed, is as an uncoiled spring,
A built-up power that does not yet have aim,
But furiously will shoot at any thing,
And then, when spent, the Bull is once more tame.
So down and up, first bound, then free, plods he,
Obeying the law of periodicity.

3   Gemini, the Twins

Bisect the Bull-ring; cut it into two;
A pair, the left and right, are born: the Twins.
Straightway there are two diff'rent points of view;
Straightway they push; and so the circle spins.
And when it spins there is a rush of air,
Which is the very birth and start of sound,
And soon are talking glib the merry pair;
Fast flows the chitter-chatter, round and round!
And yet this is of reason the true birth,
For reason has with ratio closest link,
Which both to have you must bisect the earth,
And make compare; this is the power to think.
This same comparing power, although Twins' pride,
Is weakness, too; they just cannot decide!

4   Cancer, the Crab

Two halves there are that 'gainst each other press,
And here is now the fount and source of pain;
For pain is saying 'No' instead of 'Yes',
To any pressure able to constrain.
But th'half that does the pressing likes it well,
So it says 'Yes', and pleasure comes to be.
These two together, pleasure-pain, then dwell
A spinning coin, each up alternately.
The side that feels the pain is sensitive
And soft; of others' pain too well aware;
The obverse side is selfish, does not care.
Thus then the Crab, at once both soft and hard,
So friendly, yet for others small regard.

5   Leo, the Lion

No longer touring round perimeter,
Or veering hesitant from side to side;
With pleasure-pain no more the arbiter,
No need to lash with claw, no need to hide.
Here, at the centre of it all, so sure
He is the king, and this is all his throne,
Magnanimous he couches there, crossed paw,
The Lion! And all he sees he calls his own!
He's found the centre, hit the Bull's-eye square;
That first desire to manifest has won
Its way into that inner den, found there
Himself alone, sole occupant, the sun!
Kingpin is he, as anyone can see!
He bears no grudge, as long as you agree!

6   Virgo, the Virgin

Behold, self-walled, a virgin in her tower!
Forbidding vulgar outside world to enter!
So steady in relying on that power
She knows springs forth from out her own pure centre.
She cannot be corrupted, led astray,
Secure within her walls she's safe from harm.
Contrariwise, she goes her own sweet way,
Refusing even your uplifting arm!
She's loyal and reliable and brisk,
So conscious always of her duty to
Herself, and you and me (beware, she'll whisk
Up in her churn of rectitude poor you!).
The Virgin knows how best to nurse you whole,
Far better than you know yourself, poor soul!

7 Libra, the Scales

The centre having now been found and won,
A foray to inspect the flanks can start;
A series of comparisons begun,
And tabulated on the Libra chart.
Efficient is he at this occupation,
He'll make a list before you wink an eye!
(To balance ev'rything is his vocation)
Though after, carelessly, he'll leave it by.
He's affable and nonchalant and kind,
Harmonious in himself and with his friends,
So fulcrum-centred his perceptive mind,
It's never there; instead it's at the ends.
His eye for detail's so acute he sees,
Quite often, not the woodland, but the trees.

8 Scorpio, the Scorpion

Back to the centre now he goes, intent
To re-affirm that heart that is his core.
The information from the flanks is sent
To forest's dark where, deep, he lays his store.
With zeal, and sting in tail, he guards his treasure,
Attached to it with passionate devotion,
Possessing it as his, gives him his pleasure;
In secret there, he brews his magic potion!
He'll finish it and never have a doubt,
He'll work intensively without a pause,
When he decides some task to carry out,
Whenever he espouses any cause.
Suspicious, he is soon your enemy,
Devoted, though, no better friend than he.

9 Sagittarius, the Archer

As centre and perimeter have both
Been brought within control, now can begin
(And at this task the Archer's nothing loth!)
A rapid motion, darting out, then in.
First outward, as an extrovert, he'll dash,
A blindly optimistic, tactless, wit!
Then, with a quick illuminating flash,
He'll inward turn, and straight the bull will hit.
This extro-introverting movement makes
Him self-contained, and conscious of the laws
That govern self-development, so wakes
Him up to consciousness of his own flaws.
Law-knower thus, a justice-lover then,
Who's yet the most rebellious of men!

10 Capricorn, the Goat

Determined now to set upon the road
To self-development, it is the earth
That must be conquered first; a heavy load
This task imposes; there's no time for mirth!
But as a goat a mountain peak will climb
And steady, eat, absorb, what lies in's way,
So puts the Capricorn, in measured time,
The gross material world beneath his sway.
He's proud, ambitious, frequently dogmatic,
Persistent, often sad and slow to laugh;
His hand on erring shoulder is emphatic,
He does not like to do a thing by half.
Stern, upright, self-reliant, sometimes shifty,
He's often mean, but he will call it 'thrifty'!

11 Aquarius, the Water Carrier

An inner self-development's now sought,
That world that can't be seen must now be won.
As samples on a slide are pinned, and caught,
And analysed, thus is the work begun.
It's work that is so subtle, quiet and gentle,
Removed by far from market's motley throng,
It's work that's so refined, ethereal, mental,
That to it lusty actions don't belong.
As water in a pitcher perched on head,
The vase of memory with facts is brim;
This makes for lack of stride, of drive, instead
The gait is wary, sceptical, and prim.

While Aquarius works to save 'Mankind' from pain,
Unseen's the ailing neighbour down the lane!

12 Pisces, the Fish

The energy has now its circle rounded,
From deepest sleep to wide awake we've come.
The silence has been broken, trumpet sounded,
And now the fruit of all this work we sum.
But have we ended? Aren't we at the start?
Before the Aries sign where we began?
A little child asleep, no mind, all heart?
Who yet the long, long race has to run?
How can we tell? Who knows what this sign means?
Two fishes swimming both in different ways?
And don't the Piscean ask himself; he dreams
He's this, he's that; for ev'rywhere's his gaze.
So naive, guileless, still in embryo curled?
So spiritual he's overcome the world?

13   The Thirteenth Sign

The thirteenth sign is not a sign at all;
You will not find it listed anywhere.
It is the still small centre of the ball;
The eye o'the storm; and all is peaceful there.
Each sign is but one aspect of the whole,
An hour o'the clock, and only in that hour,
Fulfills its function and allotted role;
When other chimes are struck it has no power.
But the Universal Man who's worked his way
Into the 'Holy Place', from there at will,
Shines outwards from the centre as a ray
And beam of light, and any sign can fill.
Because he is identified with none,
He can, as need requires, be any one.

About Eugene Halliday

Eugene Halliday (1911–1987), artist, writer, teacher and psychotherapist, was the founder of two educational charities, the International Hermeneutic Society (IHS) and the Institute for the Study of Hierological Values (Ishval—now known as the Eugene Halliday Association).

Hermeneutics is the art or science of interpretation of texts, for example in the fields of religion, philosophy or psychology. It is the means by which these texts are examined to investigate their meaning. Hierology relates to comparative religion, being the study of sacred writings or scripture, and the principles which underlie them.

Deeply versed in hermeneutics, art, religion, philosophy and science, Halliday recommended the reading of the major scriptures of the world and the works of the great philosophers. He taught that the whole visible universe is but a tiny portion of an infinite continuum of power. All worlds, from the great galaxies to the subatomic particles, are subsidiary worlds, or whirls, or whorls, of that same power. That power is omnipresent, that is, it fills all places; it moves and feels its movements—it is sentient. 'God', he said, is a short name for that which he called 'Absolute Sentient Power', or the 'Infinite Continuum of Sentient Power'. We are its activity, its whorls, its rotations. We are not separate from God.

Halliday had a theatrical background, his parents were music hall artistes. What he learned from them would have aided his ability to understand, relate and interpret the wide range of subjects he chose to study. Originally intending to be a violinist like his father, a childhood illness partially paralysed his left hand leading to a change of direction. He attended the Manchester School of Art from 1928 and in the 1930s-40s worked for Allied Newspapers as an illustrator and journalist. He was a conscientious objector in the Second World War and helped others in their tribunals. His work was shown in the Manchester Academy of Fine Art and other galleries, and he began giving talks on philosophy. Soon he became the catalyst for a community of creative people, including refugees from Nazi Germany. This led to the founding of the IHS (1959) and Ishval (1964).

From the late 1950s Halliday devoted more and more of his time to writing, teaching and therapeutic work. He taught that the highest centre of each of us is unique, and how to centre ourselves inwardly so as not to be swept off balance by the pressures of worldly life. One way of achieving this is through a new awareness of language that asks us to make our vocabulary active rather than passive by clearly defining the terms we use, through the study of etymology. His work was to help us to find ourselves, to become independent beings—including being independent of him. His aim was for all those who could rise to it, to become reflexively self-conscious.

Halliday was kind and compassionate—he was a healer whose psychotherapeutic work enabled the recovery of many troubled minds and souls. Yet he almost never gave advice, but taught people how to advise themselves.

He could be a ruthless taskmaster when he saw his students could be inspired to further development. His teaching was esoteric and profound, but also practical. He taught that our true place is in the eternal world, yet he did not despise the time-process, which he explained was essential for our spiritual development. He was a charismatic teacher who embodied the principles he taught and inspired many to follow in his footsteps.

Halliday's work was founded in Love, which he defined as 'working for the development of the highest potentialities of being'. Love, he wrote, 'is a feeling or activity directed at the development of the highest possible functional relationship between beings, an activity which contains, indissolubly bound together, elements of thought, feeling, and will, so that this activity is conducted with clarity, sensitivity, and power.'

Halliday wore his wisdom lightly and had a profound effect on everyone with whom he came into contact. More than thirty years after his death he is still held in affectionate reverence. None of those who met Eugene Halliday could ever forget him, and those who were taught by him regard him as a great sage, a true, reflexively self-conscious being, and a man of great humour and compassion.

Hephzibah Yohannan

Further Reading

Philip Rose

The Way: Spirit from the Well, ISBN 978-1-872240-42-8
(HB) and 978-1-872240-43-5 (PB), Melchisedec Press 2019

Waves of the Sea, ISBN 978-1326431525, 2015

The Beam & Beyond the Beam, ISBN 978-1291675092, 2015

For details of Philip's other works, which are listed at the beginning of this book, please email info@melchisedecpress.net

Eugene Halliday

For those new to the work of Eugene Halliday, a good introduction to his work are *Reflexive Self-Consciousness* and the first five chapters of *Contributions from a Potential Corpse*, Book I

Reflexive Self-Consciousness
ISBN 978-1-872240-39-8 (PB), 978-1-872240-40-4 (ebook)

Contributions from a Potential Corpse, Book I
ISBN 978-1-872240-03-9 (HB), 978-1-872240-44-2 (ebook)

The Tacit Conspiracy, ISBN 978-1-872240-02-2 (HB)

The Conquest of Anxiety, ISBN 978-1-872240-09-1(HB)

Essays on God, ISBN 978-1-872240-08-4 (HB)

For further information on these and other works by Eugene Halliday,

please visit: www.melchisedecpress.net

or email: info@melchisedecpress.net

About The Author

Philip Rose is an artist and writer. Born in 1925, he served in the Royal Navy during the Second World War. After demob he attended the Webber Douglas School of Dramatic Art and became a professional actor. For ten years in the 1950s and 1960s he and his actress wife Elizabeth ran their own puppet theatre, writing their own plays and making all the puppets.

Following the war's end Philip fell into a tremendous depression at the state of the world. Atomic bombs had been dropped on Japan sending the world into a state of shock. The fallout cleared to reveal the Soviet Union and America facing each other with enough nuclear weapons to blow up the earth. Being a creative person with many questions, Philip began writing plays, drawing on ancient texts such as the Tao and Vedanta, in an attempt to sort out the world's perilous situation in his own mind.

Meeting Eugene Halliday in 1950 had a profound effect. Here was a man who knew all the works Philip had been exploring and could answer his questions. He offered Philip a new way to view the world, a new understanding, which has remained with him ever since.

Philip has been a deep sea yachtsman, who has sailed over 30,000 miles of the seas and the oceans of the world. A member of the Royal Naval Sailing Association, the Hakluyt Society and the Instow Yacht Club, he taught Navigation for many years at the Bideford School of Art, made his own navigation instruments by hand, and wrote the practical guide, A Primer of Celestial Navigation (2006).

He ran, with his wife and daughter, a studio in Westward Ho!, North Devon, for over forty years, selling only their own work, paintings, drawings, leaflets and small models of mythical and legendary figures which they had designed and carved themselves. He is now retired — but still writing — and lives with his family in a large old 14th century house in Bideford.

www.ingramcontent.com/pod-product-compliance
Lightning Source LLC
Chambersburg PA
CBHW051028030426
42336CB00015B/2769